DREAM
Achievers

50 Powerful Stories of People Just Like You Who Became Leaders in Network Marketing

———◆———

Insights, Tips and Advice from the Pros to Help You Stay Motivated...

...and Find Your Dream at the End of the Rainbow

———◆———

Anthony and Erik Masi

Dream Achievers

Anthony & Erik Masi

Copyright©2001 by Anthony & Erik Masi
ISBN 0-938716-62-X

Published by
Possibility Press
One Oakglade Circle • Hummelstown, PA 17036
Phone: (717)566-0468 • Fax: (717)566-6423
e-mail: PossPress@excite.com
Visit us on the Internet at www.possibilitypress.com

Manufactured in the United States of America.

*The facts in the profiles presented herein
are as reported to the authors.

DEDICATION

We dedicate this book to our parents,
Frank and Helen, for their unconditional
support in every dream we chase.

Other Books by *Possibility Press*

No Excuse!...Key Principles for Balancing Life and Achieving Success
No Excuse! I'm Doing It...How to Do Whatever It Takes to Make It Happen
No Excuse! The Workbook...Your Companion to the Book to
Help You Live the "No Excuse!" Lifestyle
Reject Me—I Love It!...21 Secrets for Turning Rejection Into Direction
If They Say No, Just Say NEXT!...24 Secrets for Going Through
the Noes to Get to the Yeses
The Electronic Dream...Essential Ingredients for Growing a
People Business in an e-Commerce World
Time And Money.com...Create Wealth by Profiting from
the Explosive Growth of E-Commerce
Are You Living Your Dream?...How to Create Wealth and
Live the Life You Want...You Can Do It!
If It Is To Be, It's Up To Me...How to Develop the Attitude of a
Winner *and* Become a Leader
Get A GRIP On Your Dream...12 Ways to Squeeze More Success Out of Your Goals
Are You Fired Up?...How to Ignite Your Enthusiasm and
Make Your Dreams Come True
Full Speed Ahead...Be Driven by Your Dream to Maximize
Your Success and Live the Life You Want
Focus On Your Dream...How to Turn Your Dreams and Goals Into Reality
SOAR To The Top...Rise Above the Crowd and Fly Away to Your Dream
In Business And In Love...How Couples Can Successfully
Run a Marriage-Based Business
Schmooze 'Em Or Lose 'Em...How to Build High-Touch
Relationships in a High-Tech World
SCORE Your Way To Success...How to Get Your Life on Target
What Choice Do I Have?...How to Make Great Decisions for Tremendous Outcomes
Dump The Debt And Get Free...A Realistic and Sensible Plan to
Eliminate Debt and Build Wealth in the 21st Century
Congratulations! You're A Millionaire!...The Secrets to Selling Your Way to a Fortune
Brighten Your Day With Self-Esteem...How to Empower, Energize
and Motivate Yourself to a Richer, Fuller, More Rewarding Life

Tapes by *Possibility Press*

Turning Rejection Into Direction...A Roundtable Discussion With
Network Marketing Independent Business Owners

Dream Achievers

Table of Contents

Dream Achievers
Occupational Backgrounds

Accounting
Lydia Chan
Jeff Nicholls

Aerospace Industry
Steve Francisco (Executive)
Jim Grande (Rocket Scientist)
Rod T. Stinson (Machinist)

Airline Industry
Melba Washington

Banking
Anita Rawls (Executive VP)

Business Owners
J.K. and Becky Baker (Fabric Store)
Bob and Della Bourke (Janitorial)
Bob Gilstad (Painting Business)
Chuck Hoover (Auto Dealership)
Gary Morgan (Fitness Equip Store)
Linda Shea (Hair Salon)

Clerical
Euphiazene Linder

Construction
Chuck Hoover
Hans Johnson (Underwater Diver)

Corporate
Dale Calvert (IBM)
Bob Covino (Vice President)
Michael J. Krach (Vice President)

Education
Janet Day
Belva Flegle (Promotional Director)
Mary Griffon
Eileen Silva

Fashion Industry
Susan Francisco
Tony Kent (Photographer)
Merenna Morrow (Fashion Model)

Food Service
Shane D. Klippenes (Grocery Str Mgr)
Euphiazene Linder (Dish Washer)
Jeff Roberti (Waiter)
Carolyn Spargur (Restaurant Hostess)

Franchising
Colter C. Brinkley (Aircraft)

Government
Vicki Morgan (French Government)
Tom Shea (Assistant Director)

Homemaker
Jan Ruhe
Susan Waitley
Brenda Willoughby

Industrial
William H. Day (Coal Mining)
Dave Savula (Rubber)

Interior Design
Susan Waitley

Media
Joe Felger (Video Engineer)
Andy Willoughby (Broadcasting)

Medical
Carol Felger (Dental Hygienist)
Leslie Stanford (Dental Hygienist)
Susan Waitley (Dental)

Military
Roland Fox (Air Force)
Dave Johnson (Navy)
Ray Robbins (Major, Helicopter Pilot)

Music
Belva Flegle (Musician)

Newspaper Industry
Len Clements (Carrier)
Dayle Maloney (Reporter)
Jimmy Meyer (New York Daily News)

Pilot
Ted Morrow (Commercial)
Ray Robbins (Helicopter)

Real Estate
Bob Covino (Development)
Gloria Gilstad
Ken Pontious
Ray Robbins
Todd Smith
Sam Washington

Restaurant Owners
Bob Covino
Erling J. Schroeder

Retail
J.K. and Becky Baker (Fabric)
Bob Covino (Vice President)
Euphiazene Linder (Sales Clerk)
Gary Morgan (Fitness Equipment)
Ray Robbins (Amusement Vending)

Sales
Robert Butwin (Sportswear)
Karen Cormier (Jewelry)
Chuck Hoover (Cars)
Dave Johnson
Dayle Maloney (Recreation Vehicles)
Cindy Samuelson (Cosmetics)

Secretarial
Karen Cormier (Urology)
Belva Flegle (Executive)
Pamela Nicole Randisi (Executive)
Carolyn Spargur (Legal)
Elizabeth Weber (Legal)

Shipping and Transportation
Shirley Pontious (Sales Rep)

Sports
Len Clements (Professional Umpire)

Student
Dennis Nun (College)
Lisa M. Wilber (High School)

Teaching
Len Clements (Computer Instructor)

"Our aspirations are our possibilities."

Robert Browning

Introduction

You are about to read 50 inspiring stories about ordinary people who became Dream Achievers. They come from all walks of life, range in age from 25 to 75, have educations from high school dropout to Ph.D., and backgrounds from poor to wealthy. And, when you think about it, they're probably just like you and most everyone you know.

One thing they all had in common, though, was a burning desire—a big dream—to dramatically change their lives. And they all did it! But they didn't just get lucky or inherit their fortunes, and they don't have a special gene that makes them superhuman. They did, however, use network marketing as the vehicle to achieve their dreams.

Do you have a dream for *your* life? Network marketing is well known for igniting dormant dreams. Ask anyone who first gets into it and they will tell you they have finally found the opportunity they can use to make their ordinary lives *extraordinary*.

Unfortunately, some people give up on their dreams. Eventually, this can lead to disillusionment and sadness—they feel empty, like something is missing from their lives. They have simply settled for an ordinary lackluster day-to-day grind. These people often think success can't possibly happen for them—that it just happens for others. Furthermore, they frequently believe that anyone who becomes successful just lucks out. Sound familiar?

Many people are excited about network marketing when they first get in. However, they sometimes get discouraged if they don't succeed overnight. They may begin comparing their new venture to their regular paycheck jobs—not fully appreciating that network marketing is a business! And like most businesses or careers, it takes time to build it to become successful.

They need to understand that in order to be successful in network marketing, or anything else for that matter, it's essential to have a *dream*. They need to wake up every day with a purpose and a mission. They need to be willing to take risks, work beyond their normal hours, and deal with people challenges. They may need to spend every Tuesday night at a weekly opportunity meeting, instead of at home watching television. They may need to make phone calls every day and learn to deal with rejection and apathy. And they may need to change their "I work for someone else" thinking to "I work for me now" thinking. On

10

top of all that, they need to not let negative-thinking people steal their dream.

So how can anyone stay motivated and build a network marketing business, while working a job or running a traditional business? Well, one thing they can do is read this book!

Most of the people in this book run their network marketing businesses full-time. They have annual incomes ranging from $40,000 to several million dollars, with organizations numbering anywhere from 500 to 500,000. And that's why we call them Dream Achievers.

So, you may be asking, "What do these people have to offer me?" They're here to share their experiences and cheer you on! They've basically been where you are and will keep reminding you that the decision you made to go with network marketing was the right one. They'll tell you to hang in there and keep going because the bigger your business grows, the more excited you'll be. If you have a challenging day and feel like quitting, just pick up this book and read a story or two.

Turn to page 122 and you'll meet Dayle Maloney, a man who was over $350,000 in debt, and at the end of his rope. But as you read his story, you'll discover that since he's been in network marketing, he has paid off all his debts and is happier today than ever—*and very wealthy*.

On page 40, you will meet Lydia Chan, an Asian woman with little knowledge of the English language, who came to the United States with her young son. Even though she had nothing but the clothes on her back—and the desire to succeed—she got into network marketing and turned her life around.

And on page 117, you'll meet Euphiazene Linder, a woman with only an eighth-grade education, who was dismissed from her job at JC Penney. In spite of the health challenges that plagued both her and her husband, she is now generating thousands of dollars a week in network marketing.

An old adage says, "If they can do it, so can I." That's the attitude this book can inspire you to adopt. Even when it seemed almost impossible, these people made network marketing work for them. If you're having a challenging day, think of them and how difficult it must have been for them to rise above their circumstances. Maybe you'll come to realize that your problems really aren't so bad after all.

On the following pages you'll meet people who had profound experiences, for example, by taking nutritional products that came from their network marketing suppliers. They were so moved by their results that they couldn't stop telling others about them.

You will also meet people who wanted freedom from their jobs or other businesses. They dreaded having to commit 40 to 60 hours a week doing work they really didn't like. Now, thanks to their success with network marketing, they don't have to wake up to a loud obnoxious alarm clock, report to a demanding boss, be consumed working for someone else's dream, or feel like their business owns them—instead of them owning it.

Many of these people wanted to take better care of their families and have enough money to send their children to college. Others just wanted something to do on the side to generate some extra income. Whatever the case, you will be reading real stories about people just like you—*people who made network marketing work for them.*

These leaders also share the tips and techniques that have helped them build their part-time businesses into thriving moneymaking machines. They reveal their most effective methods of meeting new people and sharing their opportunity with them. They candidly discuss how they deal with self-doubt and rejection, how they handle and overcome obstacles, and how they successfully run their businesses. They also tell you the most common pitfalls to avoid.

These people share with you their most fulfilling moments as network marketing independent business owners, as well as some very funny stories about what happened to them along the way. But even more importantly, they tell you what they did to make their businesses flourish.

This book represents the first time in network marketing history where so many leaders, each associated with a different supplier(s), have come together to support the industry as a whole. They are true Dream Achievers!*

In your hands is the book we wish we had when we first started our network marketing business. Read it, enjoy it, learn from it, laugh with it, identify with it, and read it again. And most important of all, share it with prospects and the people in your organization. Remember, helping others succeed will help you succeed in your network marketing adventure.

It's time to start dreaming again. Now go make it happen—*for you!*

Anthony and Erik Masi

---

* *The incomes of the people presented in this book illustrate potential only, and in no way are projections or estimations of the income you could earn in your network marketing business. No company names, titles, products, services, organizations, or residential locations are given. This is done to protect the privacy of those featured, and also to prevent the book from being an advertisement.*

The Interview Questions

The following questions were used during the interviews:

- *How long have you been involved in network marketing?*
- *What is your education level?*
- *What did you do before network marketing?*
- *How did you get introduced to the industry?*
- *Is the product line an essential ingredient to a successful network marketing business?*
- *Is this company the only company you've ever joined?*
- *Were your family and friends supportive of your decision to start a network marketing business?*
- *Did you have self-doubt? If yes, what did you do about it?*
- *What were your greatest obstacles in succeeding?*
- *What is the most fulfilling part of network marketing for you?*
- *What are your top three priorities in life?*
- *How much time do you commit to your business per week?*
- *Describe a typical day/week.*
- *Describe how you motivate your downline.*
- *What value do you place on managing your downline?*
- *Do you use meetings and events to grow your business?*
- *Is everyone a potential recruit for you?*
- *What is your most effective approach when prospecting?*
- *How do you handle rejection?*
- *Do you have any special or funny moments to share?*
- *What are the keys to success in network marketing?*
- *Why do you think people quit network marketing?*
- *What advice could you give to people who are just starting out in network marketing?*
- *Now that you've been successful in network marketing, what are your future plans?*

"All of your dreams can come true if you have the courage to pursue them."

Walt Disney

J. K. and Becky Baker

"I never let results determine my attitude."
J.K. Baker

Interview conducted with J.K. only.
Background: Business Owner, Retail
Year started in networking industry: 1978

In 1978, our first year in the industry, I went to the bank to borrow some money to get my network marketing business up and running with some inventory. It seems that bank loan officers are always sitting right in the middle of the bank where everyone can hear your conversation. When I asked for the loan the banker said, "Look, J.K., get yourself a real job and don't fool with those pyramid things." I said, "This one is for real. It's a fantastic business opportunity...and oh, by the way, they have a bonus car program. Becky and I will be receiving our Lincoln Town Car in about a year." With that, he just died laughing right there in the middle of the bank and said, "I'm not loaning you any money! Even if I did, what do *you* have as collateral?" I looked at him straight in the eye and said, "You will get the best collateral you've ever gotten...*me!*"

Well, eleven months later, we got that Town Car. One day while I was driving down the road, I looked over and saw my banker in a banged up Ford Pinto. I got really excited and thought to myself, "If it's the last thing I do, I've just got to let him know this is me!"

We had just gotten our bonus car, the first new car we ever had, so I was hitting every single button I could find to get the window to go down. Well, my seat moved, the antenna went up, and everything was going crazy, but I just couldn't get that window to go down. Back then, the Town Cars had a little vent window on the side and I finally was able to get that to go down. So I stuck my hand out of that little window and started waving as hard as I could.

Finally I got his attention. He saw it was me, and as we passed I looked in the rear view mirror. He was swerving all over the road! I could see him looking back to see if it was really *me* driving that big, brand new 1979 Lincoln Town Car. It felt wonderful!

Before network marketing I was in the retail industry. I was co-owner of a chain of fabric stores and got totally busted. I lost everything. That's when a friend of mine told me about network marketing. In February of 1978 I joined a successful network marketing company, that is still around today, and I worked that business for five years until I reached the top level. I then went into semi-retirement for two years, living off the ongoing income and basically got bored. Then in 1985, my business partner and I started opening drugstores. We built a very successful chain of them in Mississippi, Alabama, and Tennessee. And during that time I was 100 percent *inactive* in network marketing!

In the spring of 1995, we got a call from a guy who wanted to talk to us about a brand new network marketing company. We had no reason to look at it. We were still receiving ongoing income from the company we were already associated with, and our drugstores were doing very well. I didn't want to hear anything about it. He kept sending me information, but I simply threw it into the trash. The network marketing company we were with had a policy that prevented us from working other network marketing opportunities because of the level we had reached. We didn't have a problem with that policy because it was in place when we joined. And since we weren't about to walk away from our ongoing income, we didn't waste our time reading what this guy was sending us.

Then, in October of 1995, a friend of ours who we hadn't spoken to in about seven or eight years, drove 12 hours to tell us about *his* opportunity. I wasn't intrigued because I thought I'd seen it all before but, when he left, Becky turned to me and said, "This company is going to be big." She saw some things that interested her, such as a potential opportunity for our two sons to build a network marketing business—so they could create the lifestyle for themselves that we were already enjoying. We spent several months researching the potential success we could have if we became distributors for this new company. We loved network marketing and thought we owed it to ourselves and our children to explore what this company had to offer.

During that time I got a notification from my bank that really shocked me. About seven years prior I had co-signed a note at the bank with my brother-in-law to help him get started in a business. He worked diligently, but as the old saying goes, "Timing is everything." Despite his efforts, the business ended up closing and he lost everything. And, since I was the co-signer, I had to pay the balance due the bank, as well as other outstanding debts—which totaled $460,000!

After our investigation of the new company, we saw the possibility of paying off that debt within 18 to 24 months by working the new business part-time. It was strictly a business decision, not an emotional one. After all, we had a lot to lose if the new business didn't work out—namely our ongoing income, from the original company we were involved with, which was $80,000 to $90,000 annually. And I'm happy to say that we became successful with the new company and soon paid off all that debt!

I never doubted myself—not even one moment, since I got into network marketing in 1978! Being in the retail business, I had a perspective most people don't have when they get involved in this industry. I always understood that if you owned just one store you worked yourself to death. But if you owned a whole chain, and earned a little bit off of each one, you enjoyed life. So that thought was always in the back of my mind. And that's what I saw in network marketing. It afforded me the opportunity to build that type of business without all the headaches of traditional businesses, such as employees, debt, rent, liability, government and other hassles.

My greatest obstacles were getting other people to understand the potential available to them through network marketing, and getting them to believe that the big picture can really happen for them. Since network marketing is a relatively new way of doing business, most people don't understand it. Therefore, we still need to overcome some preconceived ideas about our industry. But that's nothing new in the business world. Franchising had to go through the same thing.

The most fulfilling part of network marketing for me is working for myself. The lifestyle of time and financial freedom is a virtual dream come true. In fact, now that Becky and I have been successful in network marketing, our future plans involve moving to Como, Italy! I've always wanted to write a book, so we're going there to take some time off. That's the neat thing about network marketing. You know all those wild and crazy things you think about and end up going to the grave wishing you'd done? Well, we're gonna do them! In fact, I'm learning Italian right now.

I think it's fabulous seeing average people getting into this industry and really making it work. Being able to share what you have with others, and seeing people's lives change—because you have helped them see the potential good that could come out of their own work—is also very rewarding.

During the first year, we averaged about 20 to 25 hours a month working our business. About half way through the second year, we saw a great potential for our future with this new company. As a result, I decided to work out a deal with my drugstore business partner that would allow me to network full-time. It's hard to put exact numbers to the amount of time we spend each week because it became our life, by choice, I might add. We might work real hard one week and take the next one off. But if you took an average it might be around 20 hours a week, not counting travel time.

During the week I spend most of my time doing weekly meetings, one-on-one presentations, and making phone calls. I also spend a lot of time doing personal recruiting and meeting with my downline regularly.

I motivate and lead my downline by example. For instance, they see me doing meetings and recruiting. They're more likely to do what they see *me doing* rather than what I simply say they need to do.

I also make it a point to never prejudge when it comes to recruiting people. The person I'm talking to might be the worst prospect in the world, but his or her brother could be the greatest in the world!

I am a "warm market" network marketer. I work primarily off of a list I have made of all the people I know, and my approach is simple. If it's a close friend of mine, I'll make a call and say, "Hey Jim, you won't believe what I've got a hold of! What are you doing in the next 20 to 30 minutes?" If they hesitate for a moment I say, "I'm on my way!"

For acquaintances I don't know well, I say, "Becky and I have set up a dealership in this area. Would you mind if I just ran this thing by you and left you with some information so that you'll know what I'm doing? I'll be by to get all the stuff back from you in about a week. If you know of anybody who would be interested in becoming a dealer, would you please let me know?" They usually say yes. But if they say no, I respect that and move on.

I don't try to sell people anything. I tell them my story and why I am excited. I'm in and out in 20 to 30 minutes. Then, when I go back to pick all my stuff up, I gather everything together and say, "Now, if you know of anybody who wants to be a dealer, please let me know." My philosophy is if they're interested they'll say something, if not they won't. This way everybody stays friends!

I don't let rejection bother me. There have been many times that my wife has looked at me and thought I was crazy, because when people said no I would say, "Hot dog!" I realize that every no brings me closer to a yes. My point of view is to be activity-oriented, not results-oriented. My excitement and thrills come from the privilege of being able to share the business and the product. I don't care if people say no because if I continue with the activity of sharing, it will work no matter what. I never let results determine my attitude.

I believe there are four keys to success in network marketing. The first key is to have a full perspective, a complete understanding of what network marketing is and what it can potentially do for you. The second key is to have one goal in mind—a goal that keeps you motivated to do what's necessary to make your business successful. The third key is attitude. It affects your daily activity. When you are activity-oriented rather than results-oriented, a positive attitude will keep you focused and working.

The fourth key is persistence. Lack of persistence will lead to failure in this business, as it will in any endeavor. You never know who's going to sign up. If you stop being persistent and quit after 50 noes, you may think it's not working. But what you didn't know is that 51st person might have said yes and turned out to be your star distributor. It's sort of like a deck of cards. If you've turned 48 over and have not yet found an ace, guess what? The next four will be aces!

I think people quit network marketing because they try to reinvent the wheel. They take over and work it in their own way, without letting their upline work with them and teach them what to do. I see that over and over and over again. They talk to their warm market before they really know what they're doing and it backfires. If you "burn" your warm market, you make it harder to succeed. The other reason is that they don't know what a powerful opportunity they have. If they don't have a goal that's inspiring them to work every day, they can burn out fast.

My advice to people who are just starting out in network marketing is this: the week you sign up, take your sponsor with you to talk with five to ten people. When you do that, you can quite possibly end your first week as a network marketer with two or three people already in business with you.

Most importantly, don't wait! Life's too short to wait for anything. Just go out and do it!

Bob and Della Bourke

*"I believe that millions of people are
looking for network marketing;
they just don't know it yet."*
Bob Bourke

Interview conducted with Bob only.
Background: Business Owner
Year started in networking industry: 1979

In 1994 my wife and I decided that network marketing
wasn't for us. Della and I had tried eight different network
marketing companies over 15 years and, after losing a lot of
money, we threw in the towel. We just thought, "Network marketing is for other people."

Even though Della and I agreed not to get involved with another company, something inside me was yearning to give it
another go. Then, one day, a woman I knew prospected me. She
said, "Hey Bob, what are you doing Monday night?" I knew exactly what she was doing, and I got really excited, so I
immediately said, "Nothing, where are we going?" My whole inside lit up. I knew that I was going to another network marketing
presentation.

I went to the meeting that Monday, then another one on Tuesday, then another one on Wednesday. That Wednesday night I
signed up and kept it a secret from my wife! On Thursday night
Della and I went to a dinner, and some of the people there were
also network marketing distributors. Well, it finally came out that I
was now a brand new distributor. And although Della was polite
during dinner, when we got back into the car, she let me have it!
That ride home was probably the longest half-hour of my life.

Even so, I wasn't discouraged. I knew that being in network
marketing was what I wanted to do in life. That Sunday morning I
sat down with Della and explained the opportunity to her. It was
important to me that we do this together, and I'm thankful that she
came around!

In seventeen weeks, my wife and I were generating $2,000 a week with that company. The company was brand new and for no explained reason, they changed their compensation plan and our checks ceased to arrive. So there we were, again, at the feet of another failed network marketing company.

After this happened, I confess that I was disheartened about network marketing. But I knew that if the right opportunity came along it would work. It was then that a gentleman with whom I closely worked in the previous company, Steve Gray, called me up and said, "Bob, we finally found it!" And I said, "What's that?" He then proceeded to tell me all about a new opportunity and to this day, Steve and I work this business together as business partners.

What got me so excited was the product line. In all of the years I've been in network marketing, and after all the tapes I've listened to and all the trainings I've attended, I know one thing that is essential to succeeding in this industry: you need a unique consumable product. Our supplier is the sole manufacturer of a particular product. And after learning about it and what it could do for people in terms of health, I just knew this was the company that would work for me.

I immediately began holding meetings and, because of my track record of network marketing failures, every single one of my friends and previous business partners said no to my new opportunity. What's funny is that within six months all but one of them changed their minds and decided to join me in my new business!

Even though I never succeeded with any of those past companies, my dad was always supportive of me. He knew that my personality and desire to help people would eventually lead me to the right company. I have to say, he was right!

My goal was to be just as successful as all those people who I met in all those past network marketing meetings. For years I had heard testimony after testimony from successful networkers who claimed that network marketing was working for them. But I was always puzzled as to why it wasn't working for me.

I wanted a better lifestyle for Della and me and to put our retirement income in place.

After so many failures in this industry, I finally learned that to succeed in network marketing I had to stop making excuses. It was when I finally decided to work the business and hit it hard that it finally popped. I would be on the phone sometimes until one in the morning! I would call people on the East Coast first until 10 p.m. Then I would call people on the West Coast because their time zone was three hours behind!

Della says that I was so determined to make this work that many times she would bring me my dinner, set it on my desk, come back three hours later and it would still be sitting there untouched. I would forget to eat it because I was so intent on making this work! I was, finally, committed to achieving my lifelong dream.

I also realized that my fear of rejection was instrumental in holding me back all those years. My partner, Steve, didn't have those fears and he had been successful in other ventures. Working with him has really helped me improve in that area. I would recommend that any new network marketer work with someone whom they feel is a strong leader. Steve's leadership has been a blessing for me.

I simply learned to accept the rejection *before* it happens! Just knowing beforehand that there's a strong chance someone might reject me when I tell them about my business makes it easier to deal with if it happens. When you think about rejection as a very real possibility, and that it's perfectly okay for someone to say no, it's not such a horror when it happens, is it?

I have implemented a simple exercise in my training program that utilizes this little trick about dealing with rejection. I tell new distributors that their assignment is to go out and get 20 consecutive people to reject them. I know it's an odd-sounding assignment, but many of them come back saying they failed because someone would eventually say yes! As you can see, fear of rejection can be turned into quite the opposite.

I am in an industry of relationship marketing. When I was a kid, my friends used to fight a lot. But I never seemed to fall in that category. One day when I was ten, my best friend said to me, "Bob, you never fight with anybody! Why don't you ever get mad at anyone?" To this day I remember that comment. And in all honesty, I have to say that my main priority is to help people. Fighting just doesn't make sense to me!

In retrospect, it has always been my intention to help people do their best. Somehow I never adopted the "me first" attitude, and I guess that's why network marketing is such a perfect fit for me. I spend all of my time helping other people succeed and I get a kick out of it!

My day consists basically of speaking to and training new distributors. I don't really have a set schedule, meaning that I'm not in my office from Monday to Friday from 9 to 5. I just do whatever it takes and go wherever I need to go to help my distributors.

For instance, this week I'm doing trainings in Jacksonville, Miami, Tampa and Orlando. Next month I'll be in Georgia, Tennessee, Kentucky, Ohio and North Carolina. And the month after that I'm going to Boston. I'm needed in those places, so that's where I go. And if one of my distributors needs me to do a three-way call with them, I'm accessible.

I try to keep my distributors motivated with weekly conference calls and workshops, and constant recognition. The calls are thirty minutes and they feature key speakers. The weekly workshops focus on training new distributors, showing them how to continually bring new prospects into their organizations, and how to keep their new distributors working the business. But the recognition is probably the most important of the three.

Back in October of 1998, Steve and I formed a club in my group called the "One-A-Month Club." The club was based on the mathematical certainty that if a brand new recruiter brought in just one new recruit each month, and in turn helped that new recruit do the same, at the end of twelve months that distributor would have 4,096 people in their organization. Of course, we had a lot of people joining this club!

To recognize the distributors for their successes, we hold get-togethers, inviting those who are making progress in the "One-A-Month" club to come up to the front of the room. When you sponsor one person, you get a pen that has "One-A-Month Club" on it. When you sponsor two people, you get the pen and a yellow ribbon that has the #2 on it. When you sponsor three, you get the pen and a white ribbon that has a #3 on it. For four, it's the pen and a red ribbon with a #4 on it. And for five, it's the pen and a blue ribbon with a #5 on it!

When you sponsor six or more people, you get the pen and blue ribbon, along with a 7-inch tall gold chalice cup that says "Super Achiever/One-A-Month Club" on it. One woman sponsored nine people in the month of January!

Let me tell you what has happened with these "One-A-Month Club" meetings. They are now being held all across the country! Even people who aren't in my downline are holding them. This is proof that recognition is a vital tool in keeping people motivated.

I also use another technique to keep my new distributors motivated. It's called the "24/10 Plan." A new distributor who makes his or her first sale earns a $24 commission. We teach them to reinvest that money back into their business. They do this by preparing ten information packets to give to their new recruit. The new recruit in turn sends them out to ten new prospects.

What this does is give the sponsor the new duty of doing ten three-way calls with the new recruit's prospects. Of course, when their new distributor makes their first $24, the entire process starts again. In the first sixty days that I utilized the 24/10 Plan, over 3,500 information packages were sent to new prospects!

Above all, it is crucial that you get your new distributors earning checks immediately. If you can figure out how to get your new distributor to earn a check right away and to have some positive cash flow on a weekly basis, they're more likely to stay with you. I have done that in my downline and I can say with confidence that this holds true!

From the ages of 21 to 52, even though I owned my own businesses, I was never ahead of the game financially. It was always a struggle. For eighteen years I owned a janitorial service company in Michigan. Most of those years I worked by myself, but I eventually hired a staff and had 44 people working for me at one time. That experience taught me that I never wanted to do *that* again! I decided I needed a career change, so I eventually moved to Florida and spent two years trying to sell health insurance. That wasn't working so I switched careers again and ventured into irrigation. I became an irrigation contractor and installed lawn sprinkler systems for about ten years.

I spent over 30 years working my own businesses but I didn't get very far. I had no savings and very little direction in my life. Network marketing has finally set me free. I have total time freedom and the money has been a wonderful bonus. Della and I both bought our parents new homes; we bought our daughter a new Mustang and a new truck for her son; we just acquired four acres of land on top of a mountain in North Carolina overlooking the Blue Ridge Mountains; and we've already picked out the log home that we want to build there.

Even though all those things are great, they're just things that you do with money. What really matters to me is that I continue on my journey to help as many people as I can with my business opportunity.

I believe that millions of people are looking for network marketing; they just don't know it yet. The way to get them to know about it is to tell them about it. Network marketing is in tune with the times. More and more people are seeking out business opportunities that allow them to work at home. If you don't tell them about network marketing, someone else will!

Colter C. Brinkley

"Network marketing is the final frontier for human development."
Colter C. Brinkley

Background: Franchising
Year started in networking industry: 1990

I **believe network marketing is the final frontier for human development.** The reality is that the troubles most people have in their lives every day are the result of finance and health issues. Fortunately, network marketing is a business where virtually anyone can change their health and make significant income. Above all that, network marketing stretches you. It forces you to become a better person, to do things you don't want to do, to be creative and to push yourself. I knew that it would bring out the best in me.

Before network marketing I was the president of a franchise chain. It was similar to the Century 21 real estate business, except it was for aircraft. I turned it into a million dollar franchise chain. By age 26 I was profiled in *Success* magazine and various other publications.

A mortgage broker for a home I once purchased called me a few years later to tell me about a network marketing opportunity. I did not get involved with it, but tried another one instead. Ten months later I developed the fastest-growing check in the history of that company. I rose to such a high level so quickly that the company eventually hired me as a trainer.

Around that time I was asked to be a guest speaker for another network marketing company. I took a look at what they had to offer and found myself with another big opportunity. So I decided to give it a shot. Within ten months I got to the top one percent of income earners again.

After some additional research into the industry, I found the company I'm now with, as I liked what they had to offer. I thought it was perfect for me because it involved both of the things I love—training and building. So once again I decided to give it a shot. In six months I became the highest-ranking distributor.

I'm lucky because my family and friends were always supportive of me. They were confident in my business decisions. My biggest obstacle was accepting the reality that 99 percent of the people in the world are not like me! I thought everybody would want to work and be as driven as I am. But what I found is that people want the end result but most aren't willing to work for it.

Personally, I commit at least 40 hours a week to my business. A typical day begins by getting to my office very early in the morning and planning the day. Then, I get on the phone with my leaders and do what I can to help them in their businesses. I also spend a portion of my day prospecting, and working and planning with distributors. In between all that I'm writing scripts for audio tapes and writing training books on how to build a network marketing business.

Although my first priority is my family and spiritual life, my second priority is changing the network marketing industry for the better. That's why I'm so committed to my distributors. My third priority is to improve healthcare statistics in this country, and to bring more financial stability and personal growth into the lives of the general public.

To accomplish that, I use what I call the "Red Flag Concept" to motivate my group. For example, I might say to you, "You're telling me you want to succeed in network marketing and that you want to make $10,000 a month. But, on the other hand, you're telling me you don't want to drive 30 minutes to an opportunity meeting tonight. What does that mean to you?"

Red flag! That's reality. I ask them logical questions and present them with scenarios that are completely inconsistent. This shows them that their thinking or behavior is totally inconsistent with what they want the outcome to be. This is a natural process.

If I just tell them to go to meetings and make phone calls, they're not likely to do it. So I show them what they need to do. My philosophy is this: if it's not in your best interest to do it, you shouldn't be doing it.

When approaching people with my business opportunity, I use a system I call the "Interest Check System." I ask a simple question:

"Have you ever thought about owning your own business?" Then I pause. If the person says no, I move on to another person. What I just did was an interest check. If they're not interested I move on and they never know I was prospecting. But when they say yes, I ask them another question: "If I could get you some information about a home-based business that was really working for people and you really could succeed at it, would it be in your best interest to learn more?" Hopefully they say yes and that's what I'm looking for. But if they say no, it doesn't bother me. It's just not worth my brain space to get upset about it!

After all, in network marketing, your judgment can be your worst enemy. Many of the people you think will work may not. And many of the people you don't think will work may surprise you—and do it! But you can qualify people by using the "Interest Check System." Truthfully, I could probably get everyone to sign up, but the mark of a good network marketer is determining whether or not somebody is going to work. So I teach people to "qualify, don't sell."

The number one reason why people quit network marketing is because they were "sold" into the business, meaning that someone talked them into it. That's the sales approach But what's the point in signing somebody up if they don't want to work?

The second reason is that no one has explained to them what I call the whys: Why it's in their best interest to hang in there, and why it's in their best interest to go to meetings—and on and on and on. If they don't have a track to run on, they'll burn out. Successful people are only successful because they do all the things unsuccessful people don't do.

Succeeding in network marketing requires that you be extremely focused and locked into what you're doing. Be 100 percent committed. Get that snapping turtle attitude, which means you're going to bite in and not let go until you're successful. Some people get involved in network marketing wanting to create million dollar incomes, yet they don't have a plan to act on!

I have two words that will guarantee most of your success in network marketing: *staying power.* Realize that you are going to learn to become dedicated, manage your time, create a plan of action, and talk to people. The bottom line is that when you stay in and don't quit, and are constantly working to *move* forward, you will win. Network marketing is a game where everyone can win, as long as they keep going.

It's also a game where you are grossly underpaid in the beginning and grossly overpaid later. But if you quit, what has it all been worth? What if, after three years, you aren't making any money at all? But in that third year you recruited three people who wanted their dreams as much as you did, and six months later you're making $5,000 a month? Are you a success or a failure?

Stay connected to your upline and company, keep learning and growing, and working your business hard. Do all that, and success can happen for you too!

Robert Butwin

*"You make a living by what you get,
but you make a life by what you give."*
Robert Butwin

Background: Sportswear Sales
Year started in networking industry: 1984

I **was introduced to network marketing by a fraternity
brother of mine who was making as much money in one
month as I was making in a year.** I just thought that if he
could do it so could I, and I jumped in hook, line and sinker!

Unfortunately, because of my overzealous drive to succeed,
within six months, I found myself heavily in debt. I believe that
things happen for a reason and that there's a greater purpose to be
realized when all is said and done. So I learned some things about
myself. Most importantly, I realized I had to shift my focus from
being sour about the negative situation I was in, to being positive
about keeping my dream alive—the reason why I was in network
marketing in the first place.

**Before network marketing I worked in a (conventional)
family business that distributed high school jackets.** But when
people ask me what I used to do, I tell them "I was in a family
business that had too much family in the business!" There just
came a time when I had to leave the family business and go full-
time in my own. When that time came, fortunately, my family was
supportive of my decision.

The truth is, I didn't know how I was going to make myself succeed, but I just knew that if others were succeeding, I could, too. I
quickly learned that I am the person who creates the limits in my
life, and I became obsessed with personal growth. I immediately
began searching for a mentor and reading inspirational books and
listening to self-help tapes.

Over the next five years I became very successful, but I eventually decided to look for another opportunity. I had reservations about the direction the company I represented was taking and felt I could find something better. To my surprise, I went through this same cycle two more times! I eventually found the company I'm with now. I was immediately impressed with the product line, which is the foundation of a successful network marketing business. I was also extremely impressed with the leadership that the company had in place.

What drives me to succeed in network marketing is the desire to show people a way to live a more meaningful life. Have you ever seen the movie *The Truman Show?* The main character realizes his life isn't really quite the wonderful thing he thought it was, and he embarks on a much bigger quest. I feel as though I am on that same quest, and this is what drives me to make a positive contribution to as many other people's lives as possible.

There is a philosophical question that asks, "How high should a tree grow?" The answer is, "As tall as it can." How about asking this slightly varied question, "How well should a human being do"? The answer? "The best he can." If that's the truth, then I have the opportunity, every day, to help people do their best with network marketing.

I still have much more to contribute in life. The money I'm making in this industry is great, but helping people in the way I've just described is a happiness that's in a class all its own.

My day gets going around 8 a.m. I make phone calls to new prospects, as well as to leaders in my organization, until 11 a.m. After that, I go out and play basketball. I play five days a week and I love it! At 2 p.m. you'll find me back on the phone making calls to more prospects until 5 p.m. In all, I commit about 35 hours a week to running my business.

I like to teach my leaders that there is no set way to run their businesses. Because of this, I continually look for different ways to reach out and locate compatible business partners. So, recently, I've been showing people how to use the Internet to turn their home computers into money-making machines. But if someone wants to do home meetings, that's fine too. My intent is to find people who want to make a difference in their lives, and then get them up and running through whatever means they feel comfortable with.

I then make sure that I stay in their lives! I don't disappear. I continually feed my leaders with information they can use to make their businesses more successful. I send them books and tapes; I have conversations with them about life; and I do whatever it takes to empower them and keep them going. When you keep feeding the geese that are laying the golden eggs, they're more likely to keep laying them!

If someone rejects my opportunity, it's usually because their perception of network marketing is overshadowing the truth of it. They don't have a clear picture of what the industry really has to offer, or even how it works. People automatically think network marketing is sales, but it really isn't. A successful network marketer merely presents information to people. Yes, the information can influence people to buy, but your goal as a network marketer isn't to sell—it's to present the opportunity. When a prospect wants your opportunity, you won't have to sell it to him!

Now, there are times when a person will see your opportunity and it simply won't be right for him or her. That's perfectly fine. What I do in this situation is ask, "Would you do a favor for me?" They always agree and then I say, "I know that within the next few months you will come across somebody who you feel will be ideal for what we just talked about. When that time comes, would you please call me?" At the same time, I ask them if it would be okay for me to send them information from time to time, if I feel that what I have to send is appropriate. This way I can continually "drip" on my prospects over time without flooding them with too much information right away. This is a tactful, dignified approach and I've rarely had anybody say no to me.

Yes, everyone is a potential recruit for me, but the real question is, "Do I want to work with that person?" I find that the more successful I become, the more selective I get as far as who I want to work with. Remember, you choose who you work with in this industry. I love that part!

When I do decide to approach a person with my business opportunity, I have no problem being upfront with what I have to offer. I know I can make a big difference in anyone's life, so there is simply no apprehension in bringing up the subject.

I have found some of my best distributors in a wide variety of places—the gym I go to, at parties, on planes, and at health shows. I am seeing, however, a trend towards the Internet. I believe that the Internet is going to play a more meaningful role in the future of network marketing.

People quit network marketing for all kinds of reasons. But when you come right down to it, it's generally because they find it isn't as easy as they thought it would be. The fear of failure and rejection also play major roles in quitting, and that's why I do all I can to keep their enthusiasm alive. I know network marketing isn't easy but, then again, nothing worthwhile ever is! I've been where they are and I know how quickly someone can get discouraged. So I'm always there helping them to cross that finish line.

To put things into perspective, remember that people who quit are found in every industry! I've had many people quit and I certainly know that more will quit in the future. When a person quits my organization I take a serious look at why it happened. I then ask myself what I could have done differently to encourage them to stay involved and continue to go after their dreams. I do this evaluation because I want to learn more about people and what makes them tick.

But I never blame myself for the quitters! There's a saying that says, "It's easier to pull a rope than to push it." And yet another saying that says, "It's easier to give birth than to raise the dead." So if a person has stopped working toward his or her goals, or wants to quit, there comes a time when I have to step back and stop wasting my time.

The most important keys to success? Mentors, mentors, mentors! My greatest challenge in this industry was finding a group of people who had values similar to mine. That's why, in spite of my past successes, I kept changing companies. How can you grow in a company that doesn't share your vision? So, after you find a product line you love, find a mentor who shares your values and let them guide you.

I live by a philosophy that says, "You make a living by what you get, but you make a life by what you give." Adopt that same philosophy. Become a mentor yourself, and give all you can. I'm on a mission to impact the lives of as many people as possible with the opportunity of network marketing, and will continue to do so for as long as I can.

In the movie, *The Lion King,* the father lion is talking to his son and says to him, "Son, you are more than you have become." This statement holds true for so many people today. People don't allow themselves to access the potential they have, and so they settle for much less. Network marketing is a vehicle that not only enables *you* to become more, but also enables you to reach out and help *other people* become more.

Dale Calvert

"Formal education will make you a living, but self-education will make you a fortune!"
Dale Calvert

Background: Corporate
Year started in networking industry: 1980

One time I was going to Orlando, Florida, for a seminar and seated behind me on the flight were a few prominent sports people. I was putting my luggage in the overhead compartment when this lady carrying a camera came hurrying through the aisle. I really wasn't paying attention to her, but I could see that these celebrities were getting ready to have their picture taken. All of a sudden this lady stops at my aisle and says, "Dale! Can I take your picture?" And these guys looked at me like, "Who the heck is this guy?" That's when I thought, "Dale, you must have made it, my man!"

Network marketing has definitely changed my life. When I was 20 years old and working for IBM, I got two promotions early on, and quickly realized I had hit the glass ceiling. I tried to get into sales but they told me I didn't have whatever it took to accomplish that.

One day I listened to a tape that discussed the various ways you can make money, including how you could duplicate your efforts through other people. I got 100 percent sold on that concept, and started listening to inspirational tapes. My best friend, at the time, had been to a network marketing briefing and said it was great. I went to hear it for myself and realized I had found what I was looking for.

The product line really excited me. I believe that weight-loss products are a proven success because people today are concerned with how they look. I knew we had a product that really worked.

That was important to me because people in my downline would have the chance to make money quickly on a product that was in demand.

I feel fortunate because my family and friends had no problem with what I chose to do. I was so young and so fired up that they weren't able to throw water on me. When you get really excited about what you're doing, you will automatically get support!

But there were times of self-doubt. I think everyone has self-doubt in this industry. It took me a long time to get to where I am, but I always knew that if I just worked hard it would pay off. I saw the opportunity to create a six-figure income and have time freedom.

When I started my business, I lived in a little 600 square-foot house. To inspire myself, I would drive my beat up Chevette over to a really nice community where there were huge houses on a lake. I took pictures of those gorgeous homes in their beautiful settings. I'd then put them all around my house and visualize one day that I would live there too. Nine years later we bought a house there! And right now, I'm building a 15,000 square-foot home on a 100-acre piece of land.

My greatest obstacle in succeeding was not understanding that the only person I could control was myself. I could control my attitude, activity and work ethic, but I couldn't control those qualities in my downline. The biggest mistake most people make is spending too much time with naysayers and not enough time with the people who want to move on.

The most fulfilling part of network marketing for me is watching people achieve their dreams. I love knowing that I played a small part in their success. Truthfully, I don't have to work my business that much anymore. But since I'm helping people, I feel like I'm on a mission. So I put in the time.

On a typical day, I usually get up around 9 a.m. and take some time in the morning to read. Then I spend the rest of the morning and early afternoon, until about 2 p.m., making phone calls and generating leads for my key people. I enjoy the rest of the afternoon with my family and then we have dinner. After that, I spend more time with my kids and then another few hours on the phone talking to my key people again.

I motivate my downline by helping them identify their reasons for working this business. The first thing I do when people enter the business is give them a "20-Reasons" form. They need to write down 20 reasons why they're choosing to build this business. If they don't have a deep sense of why they're involved, they may not make it for even the first 90 days. And I won't spend one more second with them until that sheet is filled out.

A simple way to approach someone about my business is to share the product first and then the opportunity. I give out a 30-minute videotape and follow-up with them. I ask if they're open to seeing more and, if they are, I take them to a local meeting. It's a quick, straightforward approach.

When someone rejects me, I say, "Next!" By age 65, 95 percent of the people are going to wind up dead or dead broke. Network marketers aren't trying to change that; we're just looking for the five percent who want more out of life and are willing to work for it. I ask people to please tell me no if I'm wasting their time. I am on a mission to help a massive number of people experience the thrill of success.

I believe people will fail in network marketing if they don't get in touch with their "why"—their reason for working the business. They will also fail if they don't listen to the trainers who are showing them how to run their businesses. Instead, they only use the knowledge and skills they come in with. That would be like me walking into a dentist's office, signing an employment application, and then pulling somebody's teeth. It doesn't work that way. It takes education and practice.

There are four things you need in order to make it in network marketing. Number one is your reason for working the business; number two is a solid foundation for your beliefs; number three is mastering retailing; and number four is mastering recruiting. When you have all of those things working together, and have that duplicate in your downline, you will be a superstar in your company!

DREAM ACHIEVERS

FACTOID
1

Number of years the Dream Achievers
have been in the industry:

8%   Less than 5 years

47%   5 - 14 years

33%   15 - 24 years

12%   25 years or more

Lydia Chan

*"I try to recruit OPP people...
Open-minded, People-minded,
with a Positive attitude!"*
Lydia Chan

Background: Accounting
Year started in networking industry: 1994

***Note: We used a translator for Lydia's contribution
to this book because she speaks little English.***

In 1994 while I was reading an issue of *Forbes* magazine, one
particular article caught my attention. It showed the top ten
wealthiest people in the U.S., most of whom, ironically, were
still in a lot of debt. I then noticed that some of the people on the
list were in network marketing and had no debt. So I decided to become one of them and be at the top of the list!

When I started I had a very old car, was living with my son in a
one-room apartment, and I couldn't even afford lunch money for
him! I wanted so much to be able to own a home and drive a luxury
car and provide a better life for my son. I wanted him to have what
all the other children had, such as a bed and a Nintendo.

My son also had severe asthma and, although I had taken him to
see a lot of doctors, his condition wasn't improving. Then a friend
introduced me to a line of nutritional supplements which I had my
son take, and he got well. Since then, he has become healthy. I also
found that by introducing these products to friends, I not only
helped improve their health, I also helped myself financially!

**Starting my business wasn't easy. We had moved to the
United States from Taiwan, I didn't know anyone, and I
couldn't even speak English.** But I had to be bold. So I would ini-
tiate conversations with Chinese-speaking strangers. I found that
some wanted to improve their health and some wanted to make
more money. After I recruited them, I educated them about the

products and the network marketing concept. I then helped them introduce the products to more people so I could earn residual income.

I have 100 percent confidence in my company's products and its marketing plan because I believe it can meet everyone's present needs for money and health. If people don't join, I feel sad that they aren't going to improve their health or their wealth.

At first you need to spend a lot of time developing your network. I held a weekly meeting for my leaders to help them with challenges and to stay motivated so they could keep going. In the beginning, you will be giving more than you receive. I even used to send my son to a boarding school so I could spend as much time as possible developing my group. But, as you develop your network, you will get more in return than you are giving. Today I do most of my work primarily during the weekends.

I find my best leaders by looking for OPP people—Open-minded, People-minded, with a Positive attitude! I also look for people who are available, teachable, and faithful to this business and the product.

During the past few years I have learned that many people quit because they were misled into thinking they could make a lot of money without doing much work. That is simply not the case. Their upline needs to educate them properly about the business. They need to know the truth or they're likely to quit.

When I first talk to people I ask them how much income they would like to earn every month. There's a big difference between $300 and $10,000 a month! It takes more work to make more income. If they want to make only a few hundred dollars a month I will show them what is required to do that and so forth.

The key to success in network marketing is to have confidence in yourself, the company, and the product. You also need determination, persistence, respect and understanding of your downline, honesty, patience and fairness. Network marketing is really a course in psychology! You need to be sensitive to the needs of the people around you to make it in this business.

Len Clements

"When I get a call from somebody in my downline and they tell me they just recruited a distributor, I absolutely get more excited by that than when I recruit a distributor myself."
Len Clements

Background: Newspaper Industry, Teaching, Sports
Year started in networking industry: 1979

Before I got into network marketing, I threw newspapers out of my car at three o'clock in the morning, seven days a week. My official title was "Adult Motor Carrier." I guess that sounds better than "Adult Paperboy"! I have also held jobs as a computer instructor and a professional umpire.

Back in 1979, when I first got started in network marketing, my close friends were very supportive. In fact, I enrolled four of the first six I prospected. My family, though, has always been a little apprehensive about me doing any type of self-employment activity. They always preferred that I take the more conventional 9 to 5 job route, which they perceived to be the safer, surer way to go. Of course, now they are very happy for me and glad that I never took their advice!

I was introduced to the company I'm with now during a time when I used to write and publish a newsletter, which basically evaluated and rated network marketing companies. I did that for five years and had subscribers in many countries.

The CEO called to place a full-page ad in the newsletter but I told him I didn't run ads of that size. Since I wasn't very familiar with his company, I offered to do a review of it and requested some information. He then sent me one of every product they offer.

I was very impressed by the package and introduced it to three of my business associates who were also looking for a good network marketing program. We all joined the company within a week! I eventually sold the newsletter and now do network marketing full-time.

I always believed I'd be able to achieve success in this business, yet there have been many times when I thought the industry might let *me* down. I thought to myself, "Okay, I'm here. I'm ready. But is this really going to provide *me* with everything *I* need?" It was sort of a reversal of how most people think about it I guess. Fortunately, I wasn't let down.

For one thing, the products were superior in quality. And I immediately fell in love with three of them. The product is the primary factor that generates income, not the compensation plan. A plan can pay 10 percent down 50 levels. But 500 percent of zero products moved is zero! You need to have a genuine pride in your products because, in the long run, that's what's going to generate your income.

The thing that really got me excited about network marketing was the time freedom. There's a great ad I once read that said, "How would it feel to wake up one morning and all your bills are paid whether you roll out of bed—or roll over?" That was my hot button. Working from three to six in the morning, seven days a week for six years, definitely made me *not* a morning person! I cherish sleep! I love sleeping in as late as I want, not having to commute, and taking the day off whenever I feel like it. The whole idea of time freedom is what motivated me toward success. It's not the material things or the money so much as it is the time freedom. And I work very hard to have it.

During the peak months of February, March, September, and October, I work 50 to 60 hours a week. During the summer and over the holidays it's only about 20 to 30. Some people think 50 to 60 hours is a lot, but it's what I *want* to do. I would rather work that many flexible hours than have to work 40 fixed hours. And, as I said, if I don't want to work that many hours, I don't have to. But I *choose* to do so, and it's work I love. When I get burned out, I can stop doing it for a few days, or even weeks. It's wonderful!

A typical day starts with me sleeping in! After my coffee and reading, I'm usually in the office by 9:30 or 10 a.m. The rest of the day is pretty much spent on the phone making initial calls, follow-up calls, training calls, and three-way calls with my downline, and so forth. Then in the evening I usually do some writing. I have written a book and continue to write articles relating to network marketing. Sometimes I'll write until after midnight, but usually I'll end the day surfing the Internet or watching TV. On the weekends I do a training call and a live radio show. Other than that I go out and play!

In the beginning, my greatest obstacle was finding the right opportunity. As I mentioned earlier, I was in the business of rating network marketing companies. And, while many of them were good, many also fell short in one area or another. And, yes, I was in a few others all those years before I discovered the company I'm with now. I learned by experience that perception and reality are sometimes two very different things, in this business as well as in many others.

Seeing my distributors achieve success is the best reward in this business. That validates what I do. When I get a call from somebody in my downline and they tell me they just recruited a distributor, I absolutely get more excited by that than when I recruit a distributor myself.

I also place great value in live meetings, as they are a great place to expand your business. Guests can meet other successful distributors and get a complete overview of the opportunity. Live meetings have created success in this business for over 50 years. It just amazes me when I see competitors bragging about how they don't have meetings. But that usually means they are at a disadvantage.

People sometimes say this is a business for everybody, but it isn't. One time I was calling a prospect and the phone rang in a state penitentiary. They had to call the prisoner to the phone! So the word everybody isn't entirely accurate. Basically, I look for people who have a good speaking voice and phone manner. And if they don't have it, they certainly can develop it. But that's a good quality to look for and it would certainly be an advantage in starting out. And obviously, enthusiasm is very important too.

I also look for people who are teachers. They often make much better network marketers than professional salespeople. The whole object of network marketing is to have people duplicate what you do, and teachers already know how to teach!

When I approach prospects, I simply tell them the truth. I let them know that it's hard work and it takes a lot of time. I lay it on the line like that because their reaction is, "Wow, you're the only guy who's told me the truth. This other guy said I was gonna get rich in three months handing out tapes." We're talking about credibility here.

When I tell them the truth about the negatives, it establishes trust. So when I describe the benefits of my opportunity to them, the positives become far more credible as well. Although, to be honest, I do sometimes place myself at a marketing disadvantage with this approach because I can easily be out-hyped. However, I know those folks will learn the truth sooner or later. And when they do, they'll remember the ones who were honest and realistic with them the next time around. And I want to be the one they remember.

In the beginning, rejection bothered me. I'd let one no ruin my day. Today, it just doesn't matter to me. They're not saying no to me or the opportunity—they're saying no because they don't know! I don't mean they're stupid, they just ignore it because they don't understand what they're saying no to. There are 263 million people in the U.S. alone who are not in network marketing, so you're never going to run out of people to talk to!

The number one key to success in network marketing is to have a laser beam focus on one company and commit to it for at least a year. If you were to make a list of the most successful network marketers in this industry, most have been in only one company for years.

Those who quit the industry do so for one of two reasons: Either their expectations were not met, or somebody else created a greater expectation. Most of the attrition in this industry could be completely avoided if distributors would just tell their guests what to expect from the very beginning.

Do your research before you make a decision. So many people jump into the first company they see because they've got nothing to compare it to. So once you finally find the company you're passionate about, be a monogamous network marketer.

Put the blinders on, focus on the company, and have at least a one-year commitment to it where you give it your all. Follow your dream and do whatever it takes, and your success is sure to come!

Karen Cormier

"When I fully understood the concept of network marketing, I couldn't figure out how it couldn't *work."*
Karen Cormier

Background: Sales, Secretarial
Year started in networking industry: 1989

Time freedom is definitely the most fulfilling part of network marketing for me. Oh, how I enjoy my freedom! My dad is 93 years old. This past summer I spent time with him fishing, which he loves to do. When you can take your 93-year-old dad out fishing anytime you want, and not have to be on the job, that's a freedom most people never experience. So that's the most rewarding part of network marketing for me. Sleeping in isn't too bad either! Being back in an office would make me feel like a prisoner.

The nice thing about network marketing is that you work very hard the first year or so, but that sets up your on-going income potentially for the rest of your life. I did hundreds and hundreds of presentations during that first year—not just one or two and hoping for the best. This business has turned into a million dollar enterprise for me. Think about that! Just by sharing products and giving presentations and mastering the basics of communication, you can have all the things you want. Treat this business like a business, work at it consistently every day, and attack it! And last, but not least, it's okay to make mistakes.

Before network marketing I worked in a home-based jewelry company for ten years. Prior to that, I worked as a secretary in a urologist's office. And before that, I worked for seven years in a financial institution. And it *was* an institution!

The woman who owned the jewelry company I was working for was under a lot of stress, and started taking a line of nutritional products that made her feel better. At the same time my husband wasn't feeling up to par, and she thought he could benefit from the products as well. My job was to host jewelry parties and she thought I could take the nutritional products with me to those parties and talk about them too. So that's what I did. And in four months I was making as much in the network marketing business as I was in my jewelry business. I had to call her to tell her she created a monster! So naturally I went full-time in network marketing!

I believe it's important to represent a product that gives people results they can see and feel very quickly. Then they talk to others and their recommendations to them are really advertisements that fuel the business. For example, we have introduced a product that has been clinically proven to improve your immune system. It has excited a lot of people and therefore is a significant factor in the success of all the distributors in my company. So, an excellent product is a key element to selecting a network marketing company.

I don't know if I was naive or not, but when I fully understood the concept of network marketing, I couldn't figure out how it *couldn't* work. I have always been very driven to work towards goals and feel as though I've conquered them. And once I was introduced to my company's compensation plan, I was unstoppable.

My driving force, even in my past jewelry business, has always been to win the trips that were offered as incentives! I've never missed a trip during my ten years in the jewelry business and in all my years in network marketing. Even now that I can afford to go wherever I want, I still work to win the trips!

My greatest obstacle has always been the fear of rejection. I'm a very soft-hearted person and I don't take rejection well. I also had to overcome the obstacle of the telephone.

To this day, I still hate rejection but I'm getting better. I live by the motto "Feel the fear and do it anyway!" Remember, 99 percent of the people who reject you are people who couldn't care less about you and your family or your business. One of our company's trainers told us a story that will stick in my mind forever. He said, "Why let these people ruin your business? If you died tomorrow they would say, 'Pass the salt.'" In other words, you would be letting people who couldn't care less about you, ruin your business! So, with this in mind, rejection is a lot easier for me to handle.

My phone has finally become my friend and is truly my secret weapon. During a typical week I work about 30 hours, making about 70 to 100 calls. That's mostly calling new prospects, but it also includes calling my downline. It's a lot of calling and following up with people, but it works!

My best approach when talking to new prospects is to ask them if they've ever heard of my company. It's the easiest way to approach people and open the door for a conversation. When they say yes, I say, "Well, we carry a product that may help your problem," or "your son's problem," and so forth. I endeavor to get the product in their hands.

If they say no, I say the same thing! I also give them some information and tell them I'll get back to them in the next few days. And when I'm talking to someone about the business opportunity, I say, "This is an easy way of making an extra thousand dollars a month and I can show you how." If they say that they don't have enough time I tell them I didn't think I had enough time either and, again, I offer to show them how. It's challenging to approach people when you don't know what to say, but once you know, it's not hard at all.

I also travel about 350 miles a week to run meetings. That may sound like a lot, and it is, but they are so integral to our business. We hold them every week. There's nothing like being in the same room with hundreds of people who have the same love and conviction for a product and company that you do. It's really an emotional experience and I never want to miss being a part of it.

One time I was giving a presentation to a prospect who had great potential and I was very excited about talking to her. I was telling her that I had run a jewelry business for ten years and then I excused myself to go to the bathroom. When I looked in the mirror I noticed that I had two different earrings on! When I got back to the table I said, "Why didn't you tell me I had two different earrings on?" She said, "Well, you were the one in the jewelry business for ten years. I thought it was the new fad!" It must have looked so funny.

Another time, when I first started in the business, I opened the mailbox one day and there was a check for me from my company for $8,000. I just knew it had to be a tremendous mistake, so I sent it back. They ended up telling me that they were running a big contest for the top three recruiters in North America and I placed second! I hadn't even known about it!

The magic ingredients needed to succeed in network marketing are commitment, sincerity and product knowledge. To succeed in anything, being committed is absolutely essential. Knowledge doesn't mean you have to be an expert, but you need to be able to know enough about your products so you can talk about them and get people interested in them. But the biggest kept secret in network marketing is the key of consistency. A little bit of effort every day pays off in a big way.

A lot of people quit network marketing because they have the misconception that they only need to sponsor a few people. In a sense, that's true, but those people have to be the *right* people. You can sponsor three people who do nothing or three people who go crazy and make your business explode. I heard a trainer explain recruiting once and he said it was like taking a funnel and putting it into the top of a bottle. If you put a couple drops of water down the funnel, the bottle won't fill up. But if you put lots and lots of drops in the funnel, it's just going to flow after a while and the bottle will fill up. That's how you need to look at recruiting. All the drops add up to great amounts!

Bob Covino

*"Finding your hot button will
keep you off the couch!"*
Bob Covino

Background: Corporate, Real Estate,
Restaurant Owner
Year started in networking industry: 1989

People consume over seven trillion dollars a year on everything from cars to Q-tips. Once I understood the concept
of people changing their buying habits and redirecting
their spending to become wealthy, I knew this business would
work. The success and thrill I've found with network marketing
beats anything else I've ever done. In the corporate world I was
vice president for a large retailer. From there I opened a restaurant
and a liquor store. After that I was in real estate development, syn-
dication and commercial brokering.

In the late '80s I was into luxury home building and decided to
build one for myself. The economy was perfect for buying, building, and selling, and we built an 8,200 square foot home, which we
still live in today. It has 17 rooms and seven baths. It's a great
house. I had purchased a large-screen TV for a room in my house
and this 24-year-old kid came in to set it up. He worked for a large
appliance dealer, and we chit-chatted a little bit while he was tuning
the set. On his way out the door he asked me a question that
changed my life: "Do you ever look at other ways to make money?"
I was skeptical. It felt kind of crazy actually, but he gave me an audio tape and didn't say much else.

He then introduced me to an orthodontist, for credibility, who eventually came and sat down with me at my kitchen table and showed me
the business. My wife was very skeptical and didn't see the opportunity
that night. She raised the issue about why an orthodontist would be in
business with a TV tuner. But I was open to the whole thing because I
was looking for an opportunity. Three years later I was one of my sup-

plier's top-level producers. I retired at 44, sold my three companies, and it's been a sleigh ride ever since! In fact, we just recently purchased 12 acres and we'll be building an estate.

To be honest, my family had no interest in network marketing. There was a *need*, but no interest. I didn't have success with any of my family or friends. I pretty much built my business with strangers. But even after my success today, the people who didn't join when I did still aren't involved in our business. One of them is our gardener, one is our pool man, and one still takes care of our five vehicles. We made up our minds that not everybody was going to do this. We still don't have any family members involved. They know what we do and are aware of our lifestyle. But I guess the more successful you become, the more intimidating you can be. Of course, the word effort can be quite scary to some folks!

Despite their skepticism, I never had self-doubt. I know that if I put forth effort in anything, I can make a go of it. It was difficult for me, at first, to put my faith in a couple of strangers who kept telling me they would help me succeed at this business. That was a little hard for me to swallow considering the small start-up cost of becoming a distributor. I agree with the "buyer beware" philosophy. There must be thousands of scams in every industry. But once I realized who I was dealing with and the integrity of the company, any doubts I had disappeared.

Network marketing opened my eyes to the fact that, although I thought I was successful, I didn't really have it all. The thing that I was always proud of was that I developed a pretty good lifestyle, but with three young kids, who were six, eight, and ten, I forgot to develop a life. I used to think they had sleeping disease because when I left for work in the morning and got home at night, they were sleeping!

Yeah, I lived in the big house and had the Jag in the driveway. And although I looked and smelled good, I was missing the most important years in my children's lives. I saw them getting older and envisioned myself at their weddings looking at my wife saying, "This is terrific, but where did the past 20 years go?"

When I first started, I was running three companies so I didn't have much time to work my new network marketing business. But I grabbed any hour I could, when I could steal some time from my other businesses, to work this one. In the beginning, I managed to squeeze in about 20 to 25 hours a week. But today, now that I've built a residual income, I spend only about 10 or 12 hours a week. Thankfully all of that hard work has paid off. Spending time with my kids was the missing piece to my "perfect" life, and I now have that too.

My number one priority is my relationship with the Lord, number two is my family, and number three is the ability, with my business, to go out and change some lives. That sounds pretty heavy, but that's what this business does!

Our office is in our home so it's nice to wake up, grab a cup of coffee, take a dip in the pool, feed the koi, and ease into the work day. A lot of our days are really very free. We're into boating and have a large boat on the river. In the summer we'll take distributors who have hit certain levels in the business, and we'll go for a boat ride around the city. We love spending time with them, and it also helps build their dreams.

Most of our business building is done at night. I do about five meetings a month in hotels, and we have many one-on-one meetings, kitchen table meetings and the like. But most of our time during the day is spent with our family.

My greatest obstacle in succeeding was the frustration that came along with the rejection. It occurs when you present this to people who need the opportunity desperately, whether it's financially, socially, spiritually, or whatever, and they're still not willing to give it a shot. It's a challenge you go through, but we believe every no gets you closer to a yes.

When we first got involved in the business, the rejection was hurtful and it made us angry. But today my wife and I laugh. The people who said no years ago now see the limousine, the drivers, the gardens, and all of our "stuff." We have to laugh because their lives haven't changed. They're still leaving for work at 6 a.m., putting their kids in daycare, and coming home late at night. They're only living with the trappings of just existing. Yet, they're still not willing to come over, knock on our door and say, "Hey, a few years ago when you got involved, I was closed-minded. I can see what you've accomplished today. Would you show me how you did it?"

I use a timesaving approach when sharing my opportunity with my prospects. Utilizing our business's contacting materials—the tapes, videos, and books—is a great way to share the opportunity without having to do anything except get them into my prospect's hands. Striking up a conversation is also a method I use. When people ask me what I do for a living, I say, "I help people develop their own businesses for fun and profit." That makes them curious. When they ask "What is it?" I say, "I'm glad you asked. I have some information I'll lend you. I can't promise you anything, and I'm not even sure you'll qualify, but review this info. Here's my business card. We'll get in touch in a couple of days and if you're curious, we'll grab a cup of coffee and I'll show you what I'm doing." It's basically a simple approach. I tell my distributors to relax because the key is to be sincere and not sound like a salesperson.

Even though people still reject us, we think everyone is a potential recruit. I don't care what company you're with, it's important to share your opportunity with anybody and everybody. We learned that the ones we thought would go crazy with it didn't, and the ones we didn't expect would, went nuts!

Motivating my downline is a unique process. I find out what *is* going to motivate them and then never let them forget it. Whether it's freedom, getting rid of their j-o-b, saving for college, or something else, I realize that whatever motivates me won't necessarily motivate them. That's what makes us individuals. Finding your hot button will keep you off the couch!

Once you find your hot button, upline association is paramount. The brand new person needs to have a link to someone they groove with in their upline, someone they relate to, someone who is where they want to be. That person will become the new distributor's mentor and is vital to their success.

If you're not succeeding in network marketing, it's most likely because you're fighting with that dreaded "e" word—effort. Today, society seems to have a "get rich quick" mentality. So many people aren't willing to pay the price and dedicate their time to working the plan. Also, self-confidence is a major factor to success in any endeavor. Remember these words: "If you think you can, you can. If you think you can't, you're right."

There is also a statistic, I don't remember exactly where's it from, but it states that most kids hear over 14,000 negative comments by the time they are 12 years old. So, people are more or less conditioned to have low self-esteem. Additionally, most people have stopped dreaming. Yeah, they can buy a lotto ticket and dream that they'll win big, but they won't work for their dreams because they don't know what they really want. And, if they do, they don't want it strongly enough to do what it takes to get it!

I get tremendous gratification by helping a lot of people join the party, so-to-speak. It's true that my wife and I have the toys, the boats, the Rolexes, the his and her Mercedes, the stretch limo with three drivers on payroll, the Gulf coast home, and lots of other stuff. But those are just the serendipities that come along with the success we have been so blessed with.

Over and above all of that stuff are the relationships we have formed with so many special people along the way. In fact, we just had a Covino family reunion in Pittsburgh a few weeks ago in which thousands of our downline attended. There was this sign in big lights that said, "The City of Pittsburgh Welcomes the Covino Family Reunion." The cab drivers were wondering how important this Covino guy was to have to hold a family reunion in a convention center!

Now that you realize success in network marketing is indeed achievable, my best advice to those just starting out is to check the fruit on the tree. Examine the company's integrity and then find somebody in your upline who can be your mentor. Somebody you can trust and believe in. Somebody who has ethics and morals, and will spend the time to teach and guide you. You need that link to a strong upline.

With a mentor in place, and when you work hard for however long it takes, you will succeed.

William H. and Janet Day

*"Enthusiasm dies when there's
no direction to take it in."*
William H. Day

Interview conducted with William only.
Background: Industrial
Year started in networking industry: 1980

Before network marketing, I was in the coal mining industry for 19 years and didn't like it! During that time, my
sister had introduced me to the concept of network marketing. I joined her but didn't have much success. Over the next decade or so I was involved in four other companies. I stuck with each
one for a few years and had moderate success. It certainly was a
learning process!

In 1988 I quit the mining industry after being sick and tired of
working odd shifts and never seeing our children. I quit without any
real plans and went out and did odd jobs. I was just so burned out.
Unfortunately the bills caught up with us and our family was within
30 days of losing our home. That was about the time when we got a
letter from a long distance distributor regarding a "waterless car
wash" product that his company manufactured. Much to my wife's
dismay, I got very excited about it. The distributor sent us a bottle
of it and I tried it on my car. In 30 seconds I knew I had to take a
look at the company.

The product is the network marketer's secret weapon. It's the
most important ingredient to the success of your business. It's what
got me to pursue this opportunity. I found that it was unique and did
exactly what the company said it was going to do.

**Unfortunately, our family and friends thought it was a scam.
And, like most people, they thought I was stupid for getting involved.** But they certainly feel different today! We have been able

to share some of our financial success with them, and three of our family members are now in our business with us.

I knew from the beginning that the industry was good for me, but I didn't know if I was good for the industry. Yes, I was scared and had some self-doubt. But as I got a little experience dealing with people, I got a clearer understanding of network marketing and got better at it. I sort of had a timid background. I wasn't outgoing with people and didn't assert myself enough. I was a slow starter and didn't have much self-confidence. But I had a goal to save our home because we were about to lose it. I really had to make this work. I quit the mining industry because I wanted time freedom, so that also helped me get through any doubts I had.

One of the things that I did consistently to boost my self-esteem and give me confidence was to read inspirational books and listen to tapes about the network marketing industry. I had to educate and inspire myself. I didn't know what to do and what not to do and I didn't have a mentor. So I made up my mind to do exactly what those books and tapes told me to do—*and it worked!*

People think network marketing isn't a viable way to make a living, and some even think it's a scam. But what these people don't understand is that this is a very real business opportunity for anyone. And it brings rewards greater than any other career you could possibly have. On a constant basis, we see people reaching the same plateaus of success that we have reached. Just seeing one other person attain time freedom, and knowing that we are a part of it, is extremely fulfilling. It's proof that this industry changes people's lives for the better, both emotionally and financially.

When we're recruiting, we look for people who are dissatisfied and looking for a change. We find that the 25 to 45 year old age group has a lot of those kinds of people!

I'll give you a scenario of how I would approach someone about our business. I'm sitting in a restaurant and I'll overhear somebody complaining about where they work. I'll walk over and mention that I couldn't help but hear them talking about their dissatisfaction with their job, and then I'll strike up a short conversation with them. I'll find out a little bit about them, and if I like them I'll give them my business card and get theirs in return.

I'll invite them to listen in on a conference call and point out that the number is on the card. That's my best approach and I have recruited many people that way. I like it because it's short and simple and there isn't a lot of talk. The third-party approach is my favorite. The more you do it the easier it gets.

Initially, I would defend the industry by trying to convince the people who have rejected me to reconsider their decision. But today I know that's a waste of time. When someone gives me a rejection, I say great, let's keep our friendship and then I move on. People say no. It's built in and you need to respect that.

I went full-time the first day I started because I needed to make money fast. I love meeting people face-to-face and giving one-on-one presentations. So, in the beginning, I devoted at least eight hours a day talking to as many people as possible. Today I do it about four or five hours a day, not including the phone calls I make. I work half-days on Saturday and never on Sunday.

One time I was giving a product demonstration using our premiere "waterless car wash" product on this very wealthy guy's black Lamborghini. I had set the bottle on top of the vehicle and it slid right down the hood, hit the ground and exploded! We were both wearing suits and we both dove for the ground because it sounded like a shotgun. There was white stuff all over us—the ground, the car, everywhere! I thought I really blew the presentation but the guy got up from the ground, brushed off his suit, smiled, and said, "You know what? That was the funniest thing that's ever happened to me!" Then he joined my business!

One of the reasons why I got involved in network marketing was to wake up with the birds! When the sun comes up and birds start chirping, that's when I get up. I make prospecting calls from about 8 to 10 in the morning. Then, from 10 a.m. to 2 p.m., I'm running appointments with my distributors. When we're finished, I come home to have dinner with my family. After dinner I'm back on the phone from 8 to 9:30 p.m.

I use the company's voicemail system to communicate with all of our distributors. I like to leave messages for them that summarize key points from motivational books. But I also keep in touch with our frontline leaders on a frequent basis.

A lot of new network marketers make the mistake of managing their downline. About a year or so into the business I started to do that, but it doesn't work. In network marketing you need to be a good leader, not a managing boss.

The best way to help your downline is to teach them how to give one-on-one presentations and encourage them come to monthly trainings. I go to all of the events my company offers and haven't missed one in six years! The meetings are what I attribute our success to. Our business couldn't have become successful without them.

There are a few keys to success in network marketing. Number one is integrity. Two is humility. People don't like self-serving people, so if they think you're in it for yourself, it's unlikely people will be attracted to you. The third key, and perhaps the most important one, is learning and developing people skills. Read self-help and motivational books and listen to tapes every day to get educated and confident. This book is a fine example of what can be achieved when you set your mind on something. Any type of motivational book will do. I have a library of over 500 of them! Remember, leaders are readers. If you don't stay motivated, you will have trouble succeeding.

Nine times out of ten, a new network marketer quits because of a lack of mentorship. They're fired up and ready to go. But they burn out fast when they don't know what to do. In addition to keeping self-motivated, they need a strong upline. They need someone who can work closely with them—especially during the first few months. Enthusiasm dies when there's no direction to take it in. If a new person doesn't have that support, they're lucky if they last a month. What's worse is that they're scarred for life in regard to network marketing—because of that one bad experience.

If you are new to this industry, get your hands on as many books and tapes on network marketing as possible. Keep that enthusiasm going! And don't try to "reinvent the wheel." There's nothing to figure out in network marketing. Just do the necessary steps to make it work, and don't deviate from them! You will succeed!

DREAM ACHIEVERS

Education levels of the Dream Achievers:

98%	Graduated high school
45%	Graduated college
17%	Started college but didn't graduate
2%	Started high school but didn't graduate

Joe and Carol Felger

"This business is all about human behavior. Our sponsor told us that if we could just understand that, we'd make it a lot easier on ourselves."
Joe and Carol Felger

Background: Medical, Media
Year started in networking industry: 1992

Q: **What did you do before network marketing?**
Carol: I was a dental hygienist for ten years.
Joe: I worked in TV and theaters as a video engineer for 26 years.

Q: How did you get introduced to the industry of network marketing?
Joe: Carol and I were running a campaign for a friend of ours who was running for a state representative position. One of the young men who had come to work in the campaign was a distributor of the company we represent.

Q: Were your family and friends supportive of your decision to start a network marketing business?
Joe: Some were, some weren't. There was some negativity.
Carol: The negativity, we think, came from their misunderstanding. But we really can't throw stones because we didn't understand network marketing either, before we were introduced to our company.

Q: Did you ever have self-doubt?
Joe: No. Once we looked at the product and saw what it did, specifically for my mom and Carol, we knew right away that we were sitting on a gold mine.

Q: How did the products help you?
Joe: I'm a very healthy guy; I ski and run. But after using these prod-

ucts for about a week, I noticed I was handling stress better and my afternoon lags were disappearing. But the biggest thing was that my symptoms of hypoglycemia were being alleviated. So I was totally convinced about the products after that first month.

Carol: I started using the products when Joe told me about the energy boost he was getting. Soon after I began taking them I, too, wasn't getting tired in the afternoons anymore. I felt mentally sharp in the mornings. I even stopped drinking two pots of coffee every day. But after about three or four months I also noticed I was getting dramatic relief from my lower back pain from a previous car accident. That impressed my chiropractor so much that she got on the products and eventually became a distributor.

Joe: To be blunt, we love these products so much that we would still be sharing them even if there were no remuneration. How many people told their friends about the movie *Titanic* even though they never made a dime from the movie producers? That's how we feel about our products.

Q: What was your driving motivation to succeed in your new network marketing business?

Joe: Carol and I wanted to be together.

Carol: We were two ships passing in the night. I was working days and Joe was working nights, holidays and weekends. We were just looking for freedom so that we could be together.

Q: What were your greatest obstacles?

Carol: The biggest learning curve we had to get through was understanding that timing is an issue in people's lives. When they turn down the opportunity it's because it's not the right time for them. This business is all about human behavior. Our sponsor told us that if we could just understand that, we'd make it a lot easier on ourselves.

Q: What is the most fulfilling part of network marketing for you?

Joe: The relationships we've built with people, as well as the ability to make a difference in their lives. About two years into our business, two of our distributors were about to lose their home.

They had spent their entire life savings on a home-based company they were trying to build, and it was failing. We started working with and teaching them what we learned from our sponsors. About year and a half later, they won a company trip because of their progress. When I saw them and their two kids go on the trip, at that moment I realized that this is what Carol and I were destined to do.

Carol: When it's all said and done, what you take to the grave are your friendships and the legacy you leave behind. Network marketing has allowed us the opportunity to make incredible friendships and we're so thankful for that.

Q: Describe a typical day.

Joe: This is a passion business. When we first got started we made a list of everyone we knew and set up times to meet with them so we could tell them about our business opportunity. Our sponsors came with us and talked to the people on our list. Through that Carol and I learned how to do our own presentations. For the first three years we worked our business aggressively. We still work consistently and, although we can retire financially, we've developed an income that allows us the freedom and lifestyle we never had in our jobs. We spend most of the morning making phone calls to our distributors and doing three-way calls with them. Then we go work out and have lunch. We spend the rest of the afternoon doing some more three-way calls with our distributors and then we go have dinner. And in the later hours of the evening you'll find us back on the phone doing three-ways again.

Q: Describe how you motivate your downline.

Carol: We don't. We just find motivated people! That may sound cold, but we think that's an easier approach than trying to create the sparks in people. There's a saying: "When the horse is dead, get off!"

Joe: Our job is not to be motivators. It's to lay out the hope. We look for people who want to change their lives, are teachable and willing to work, and have integrity.

Q: Is everyone a potential recruit for you?

Carol: We approach everyone and treat everybody the same. But pretty quickly we find out who the motivated people are. We call it

"The Tennis Game." We hit the ball into their court and if the ball comes back you're playing tennis!

Q: What is your most effective approach when talking to people about the business?

Carol: Being real with them and talking from the heart. This is a business about sharing something you believe in with the people you love.

Joe: We lead with the business and then validate with the product.

Q: How do you deal with rejection?

Carol: We just go on to the next person.

Joe: There isn't anyone in the world who wouldn't want to be where Carol and I are right now. I don't care if you're the president of IBM, you don't have the lifestyle that we have. They just don't know what this industry can do for them. That's the issue . . . they just don't know.

Q: How much time do you commit to your business per week?

Carol: We worked very diligently our first three to four years. But today we don't work half as many hours. The beauty of network marketing is that your organization grows and grows when the products you represent are outstanding, and the compensation plan rewards you for helping others succeed. And as your organization grows, so does your income!

Q: Do you use meetings and events to grow your business?

Carol: Yes, we built our entire business using those meetings. We have one meeting a week where distributors can bring their guests to hear about the opportunity and products. We also have a Saturday training meeting that distributors can attend to learn the nuts and bolts of the business. Our company has a tremendous support system and we take full advantage of it to help our distributors become successful.

Q: Do you have a funny experience that you could tell me?

Joe: We have so many! This business can be a riot.

Carol: One time we were telling this woman about our business and I mentioned that Joe and I were making approximately $40,000 a month. The woman said, "Is this all you do?" I was so tempted to say, "Well, no, Joe also has a paper route," but I kept a straight face and just said yes. I understand, though, why somebody would ask that question. I mean, it just sounds too good to be true.

Q: What are your keys to success in network marketing?
Joe: Number one is to find the right company with the right product and the right compensation plan. You also need to have a strong work ethic and be teachable. Just do what your upline tells you to do, keep learning, stay focused and work consistently.

Q: Why do you think people quit network marketing?
Joe: What's nice about network marketing is that it costs so little to get involved. But the problem is that because the initial layout is so small, most people don't value it. It's easy for them to walk away when things aren't moving fast enough for them because they don't feel like they're risking much.
Carol: People also quit because they just don't understand the scope of this industry, and how it can grow beyond what you could ever expect. But there is a certain amount of vision and belief that a person needs to have before they can really see that.

Q: What advice could you give to people who are just starting out in network marketing?
Carol: Find a company you're very passionate about, learn all you can and share it with people straight from your heart. Make a list of names of everybody you know and contact them all with the help of your upline.
Joe: Believe in yourself, be teachable and don't let anybody steal your dreams!

Belva and Dick Flegle

"I was 70 years old when I started out in net-work marketing, and I've never been so excited over anything I have ever done before!"
Belva Flegle

Interview conducted with Belva only.
Background: Education, Music, Secretarial
Year started in networking industry: 1995

When a good friend of ours shared a line of nutritional products with us, he really got my attention because we had just lost a wonderful son to cancer.** I have always had an intense interest in nutrition and I suddenly found myself with an urgency to get these products into other people's hands. It has since become my mission to share my company's nutritional products with as many people as possible.

I have worked as an executive secretary, a promotional director at a Christian high school, and as a secretary for the Billy Graham Association. Both my husband, Dick, and I have degrees in music. We even traveled for 11 years for our college. But nothing in my life has compared, emotionally and financially, to the success we have had in network marketing.

I jumped into this business because of the products. The more I used them, the more excited I got. They worked! My husband and children have been my greatest supporters. Dick is my accountant and loves to deposit our checks in the bank! I read in a book once to "find those who know, love and trust you," and that is exactly how I've built our wonderful business.

I never had any self-doubt. I've always felt I was helping others, which shifted my attention from doubt to making my business work. I love using and sharing our products, and when you love something you don't doubt it. And even though I had to borrow money to get started, I paid it off in three weeks by selling all of my products!

I was 70 years old when I began, but I've never been so excited over anything I have ever done before.

I am on a mission to provide as many people as possible with the very best in nutrition. I love people and really didn't think too much about the money. To be honest, I had no idea of the financial potential of this industry, but in my second month I made $2,095. It was then that I decided to go over the marketing plan!

The most fulfilling part of network marketing for me is the many wonderful new friends I have made who have become a brand new family to us. I love people! It is most rewarding to see people's lives change both physically and financially. Dick and I have great joy when we see our distributors succeeding!

Every chance I get I do my best to help someone succeed. My day usually starts with the phone ringing. It's a wonderful sound! I'm on the phone a lot providing our distributors with the help they need. I also meet people for coffee or lunch to share our products and opportunity with them. There are always lots of people to meet and call. We also mail out information to those who request it.

I motivate my downline by paying attention to them. I'm there for them whenever they need me. Dick and I have spent entire evenings talking with distributors in our home. In fact, I've built my business with muffins, cheese and coffee because once they start talking about the business with us, they never want to leave! We work and strategize with them, and help them work through their fears so they could get into a successful state of mind. The bottom line is love, compassion, and caring. With that you can't lose!

We have monthly meetings, we've done Christmas parties and product fairs, and we've been involved in a few trade shows. You get out of it what you put into it. It is work but we make it fun!

And I look at absolutely everyone as a potential recruit. Everywhere you go you find people who are sick and tired, broke, looking for work, or need something to do. I have even been on a plane and have casually taken out a brochure on my company only to wind up talking to the person sitting next to me about it! You always hear people talking about how tired they are or how they don't feel good. Every time that happens I talk about our products. I talk to everyone I can about my company.

The best way to start a conversation about your opportunity is to smile! So many people get nervous about it and, when they begin talking to somebody, it shows on their face. How can you interest someone if you look nervous or scared? So I smile! Then I share my story. I say, "Dick and I have found something that has been a tremendous help to us in retirement, not only physically but also financially. And we would like to sit down and share it with you." I approach them directly and honestly.

If I get rejected, I thank the prospect for taking the time to listen, and ask if they know someone who could be interested. And they usually do. Sometimes they will then take another look at the potential and decide to join! It's interesting how people respond. I've learned that every no gets you closer to a yes—so I just keep sharing with as many people as possible.

I put in a good 20 to 30 hours a week now, but when I first started I put in eight to ten hours a day. It was almost an addiction because I loved it. And I still do! There's nothing like network marketing!

The number one key to success in network marketing is having compassion for people. You need to want to help them and, once they're in your organization, it's important to constantly train and support them. I believe that when you make your distributors your priority, the money will be a natural outcome. Remember, the more you give, the more you receive. That's a given!

People need to be trained, encouraged, and cared about. Many quit just because they don't get those things from their sponsors or upline. Just be aware that new network marketers are often afraid to reach out and ask for help, so you may need to offer it. Also know that communication is vitally important and distributors need to know they always have access to their upline, wherever they are. For example, we always have a laptop computer so we can exchange e-mail messages with our people at any time.

My advice to people just starting out in network marketing is to find a company with consumable products that everybody wants. Their consumption causes repurchasing which produces the repeat business essential to earning residual income. You also want to be sure the company is financially stable—so you can get paid. Once you pick a company, make a commitment to work it. Also make the commitment to keep in touch with your upline. When you come into network marketing, you need to be 100 percent sure you will have the support you need to become successful.

Roland Fox

"I have a book that I wrote and it has two pages. The first page says START and the second page says DON'T STOP."
Roland Fox

Background: Military
Year started in networking industry: 1971

I was on active duty with the United States Air Force for 20 years when a gentleman in my town sent me a letter that said, "Would you be interested in a possible career-changing opportunity?" It was good timing for me, so I went and looked at it. Three people gave the meeting. They weren't well-educated, but they were well-dressed, very enthusiastic, and had a positive mental attitude. They were the kind of people I wanted to be around, so I signed up and got started right away. When the Air Force didn't promote me in December of 1972, I had no hesitancy in retiring. I knew I was going to make a fortune!

My initial motivation was to achieve the lifestyle I had as a Major and then the lifestyle I could have had if I had been promoted to Lieutenant Colonel. And even though I didn't then have the money to live that kind of lifestyle, I wasn't interested in just existing. I wanted to live the way I imagined I could. And I certainly live that way today.

Before I joined my current company, I had already tried 25 different opportunities! In fact, when I went to the opportunity meeting with my friend, it was under protest! Our agreement was that if I went I wouldn't have to hear about it from him again. So I went to the meeting and here I am!

Network marketing always seemed like something I could do. Having been trained as an airborne instructor, I knew I could teach people. So, I felt very competent. But it was the products that really got me excited. They were exceptional. They were oral health cleaning products and they could do things I have never seen done before! I wouldn't have joined if they had been mediocre.

The only clincher for me was belief. Once I fully believed in the concept of network marketing and the quality of my company and its products, I moved forward and worked really hard. When I achieved some success, I had a challenge believing other people would believe that they could do it too. Lack of belief is the only reason people don't make it in network marketing. If they knew what I know and believed what I believe, they would do what I am doing! It's as simple as that!

I love helping others realize their goals and dreams. And just knowing I play a direct part in helping them do that gives me a good feeling. After all, the only way you can become successful in network marketing is to help others succeed. Let's face it, no corporate job gives you that opportunity. Network marketing has so many good things to offer, and that's refreshing.

There are three top priorities that shape my life on a daily basis. First and most important to me is that everything I do has to be done with integrity. Second, I also value my spiritual life very highly. I follow the golden rule and do unto others what I would want done to me. I live that every day. Third, I love adventure! I love to do something different. If someone told me I could go to the moon, I would jump on the rocket tomorrow and take right off!

My day begins with a "long" commute of six feet from my bedroom to my office! I usually wake up to the phone with someone calling at 6 or 7 in the morning. I do a lot of coaching on the telephone, but we also use the Internet with our business. Every day offers unique experiences because I'm dealing with different people and situations. Lunchtime is usually devoted to an exploratory or motivational appointment. Then, about 2 in the afternoon, I take a nap. After I get up, the rest of the afternoon is spent doing conference, training, and company calls, which typically takes me up to about 10 at night.

I also speak at weekly meetings and conduct one or two weekend seminars a month somewhere in the United States or Canada. They usually last four to six hours.

People ask me how I motivate my downline, and my answer is simple: I find out if they're insane! In other words, if you continue to do the same things over and over again and expect to get different results, that's the definition of insanity. So we talk about where they are today and if they're insane. And then we discuss redirecting their work habits to get more out of life. Next, we follow up together and keep working at it.

One thing I've learned is that when training your downline, make sure you don't manage them. I place a high value on coaching. As they say in the military, "We are dealing with an all-volunteer Force here." People don't have to do, believe, or buy anything. I coach them by showing the advantages of what I am doing and how it has worked for me. Then I go through with them what would happen if they don't do it. They usually take action and keep in touch with me to coach them along—until they don't need me anymore.

Rejection doesn't bother me because I haven't been rejected yet! My *ideas* have been rejected, but I, as a person, have never been rejected. When someone says no to me, that's okay. I tell people that if they think they're here for me to convince them to earn the money I am earning, or to live the lifestyle I'm living, then they have the wrong dude. I'm not interested in convincing them to do anything. I just present an opportunity and at the end they choose if they want to do it or not. Most people have a "wall" up before they even hear you, so you need to take that wall down so people can listen.

When approaching people with my company's business opportunity, I ask them what they're passionate about and then shut up. After they tell me those things I find what I call their "seed of discontent." When I find it I say to them, "If I can show you a way to solve the problem you just told me about, would you be interested?" That's what I call "The Magic Question!" They usually say, "Of course." Then I tell them, "I will need 45 minutes to an hour of your time to present you with some possibilities. If it looks like a fit for you we'll do it, and if it doesn't, I'll thank you for your time. Does that sound fair enough?" They usually agree and make an appointment.

The ones who appear negative I will listen to for only so long. If they say, "Is this one of them pyramids?" I say, "Do you like pyramids?" I wait for their answer and no matter what they say, my response is, "Well, you're going to love this company."

Do I approach everyone? Yes! Who cares what color, race, age or sex you are? Anyone can do this. In fact, I have just recruited someone with cerebral palsy. This person is a microbiologist and knows a lot of people. And this is such a perfect business for a person with a handicap. All they need to know is how to talk. If they can do that, they can do this business!

The people who fail in network marketing do so because of unrealistic expectations. They sometimes believe they don't have to do much to become rich. If they work their job the same way they work network marketing, they would be fired! The second reason is they get some rejection and take it personally and quit right there.

Personal discipline is essential to your success in this industry. Do the things unsuccessful people aren't doing. Make those calls and travel. The closer you are to the people in your downline the more productive your organization will be. The bottom line is w-o-r-k.

I have a book that I wrote and it has two pages. The first page says START and second page says DON'T STOP. You can't lose in network marketing unless you quit. You just can't lose! Stay in action. I don't care what your action is. I don't care if you are good or bad at what you do, just as long as you keep doing it. Sooner or later something is going to happen. Just keep yourself motivated and never quit!

Steve and Susan Francisco

*"Vision is the art of
seeing the invisible."*
Steve Francisco

Interview conducted with Steve only.
Background: Aerospace and Fashion Industries
Year started in networking industry: 1985

Before network marketing, Susan was in the fashion industry and I was an executive within the aerospace industry. A friend of ours approached Susan with our company's business opportunity, and she started right away. I was the skeptical type, but she had some quick success and that really got my attention. We didn't know a lot about the industry, but we always wanted to succeed in our own business. We never thought it would be in network marketing! We just wanted it so bad that we were "ignorance on fire." We saw a lot of people having success and we surrounded ourselves with people to help us.

Unfortunately, most of our family and friends were not supportive of us. A lot of the people we cared about and loved were the biggest dreamstealers.

To be honest, we also had a little self-doubt in the beginning. We just didn't know if the potential success we were told we could have was real or not. But we started receiving some good checks and they were growing regularly. We were also making a difference in a lot of people's lives. That's when we really started to believe in network marketing.

In the book, *Think and Grow Rich*, it says to sever all of your ties and we did that. We had a "no going back" type of attitude. We *had* to be successful.

I read an article over ten years ago that said the average father in the United States spends 13 seconds a day talking with his children. But we wanted to raise our kids differently. In fact, we broke the record in our company and made the top position within two months. Today are able to spend time with our kids and live very comfortably.

The hardest obstacles for us were learning how to deal with massive frustration and rejection. The people we thought would respond well to our products and opportunity are all the ones who said no. It's kind of bizarre actually!

But network marketing is about developing leaders. It's about personal development and building a unified team with a common goal. Whenever we sit in the back of a room and watch our leaders conduct all-day trainings where they introduce us for closing comments, there is no bigger joy.

When it comes to the nuts and bolts of working the business, I am a firm believer in a daily method of operation. When I was new, I spent 80 percent of my time talking to new people about the products and opportunity. But now my typical day is spent supporting our leadership team by doing a lot of development and conference calls to drive the business.

I do a lot of traveling nationally and internationally. And even though I live in California, 90 percent of my business comes from outside the state. I go from city to city a lot, but locally we do only one meeting a month. Meetings are the best way to show people the big picture. We've always understood that facts tell and stories sell. The testimonials at the end of the meeting are the most important part. We also regularly utilize conference calling and a voicemail system.

The key to motivating our downline is constant communication. I call beginners every day for the first 30 to 90 days until they can do the business on their own. I like to work with people and support them like a workout partner would. Without consistent communication, people lose direction. And remember, especially in the beginning, you may need to believe in people more than they believe in themselves.

The people we know, our warm market, are always the best people to approach when prospecting. And we regularly seek professionals. We also look at specialty groups like the chamber of commerce, women's groups and professional organizations—even people in airplanes and hotels!

When we talk to people about our business, we ask a lot of questions and look for people's hot buttons. We got good at talking to people we knew, as well as people we *didn't* know. If you become a good listener and you listen long enough, people will tell you exactly what they want. I will ask people, "Do you have a tape player and does it work?" If they say yes, I then ask, "If I give you this tape, will you listen to it?" About 50 percent of the people who listen to the tape want to try the product. Sometimes I tell people, "I am working with a group of doctors who just developed a group of all-natural, non-drug-related compounds. Listen to this tape and tell me how you feel."

We basically get people dreaming again. We show them that if they really want success, they can have it. The most important thing is to build trust and mutual respect for one another. I spend a lot of time asking them questions about their wants, needs, and desires. At the end of the conversation I am really looking for someone who wants to run up the hill with us instead of us dragging them up the hill!

The key is to approach everyone! In the beginning I was too judgmental. Now I believe that anybody would be interested in what we have. The only reason they would say no is because they don't have enough information on our products or opportunity, or they don't understand what the whole program is about.

When it comes to rejection, you simply need to become callous to it. When you're new to the industry, you need to develop a thick skin. Quite simply, it's okay if they don't believe our story as long as we don't believe theirs! We get paid for both yeses and noes. When someone says no, we turn it backwards to spell on—and get real excited! They're not saying no to us. The timing just might not be right for them, so we don't take it personally. We teach our downline that it's a numbers game.

The number one reason people quit network marketing is because of the negative influence of family members, friends, and neighbors. They probably have little if any belief in the products, the company, the industry, or themselves. Consequently, they aren't prepared to hear the word no. What the new person doesn't realize is, there isn't any business problem that can't be solved by adding ten or 20 new people! And doing so will definitely raise their level of belief.

There are three key phases to network marketing: get people in, keep people in, and move people along. If you're working it part-time, work it with a full-time attitude and keep bringing people in. Once they're in, show them you care. Talk to them and learn about their dreams and goals. There's an industry saying: "People don't care how much you know until they know how much you care."

Finally, moving people along means getting them to the higher positions so they're earning more income. Nobody wants to be left behind. Network marketing is about people getting control of their lives, following their dreams and supporting others to do the same. But the real success comes from building relationships. With this in mind, successful network marketers need to have highly developed people skills.

Vision is the art of seeing the invisible. You need a vision and a passion for success. Nothing great will happen unless you make a decision that you are going to be successful *no matter what*. Learn the basics of the business and have a passion for it. Look at your life and figure out what is important and what is trivial. Rid yourself of all the trivial things, focus on the essentials, and work the business with integrity.

When you help other people achieve their dreams and goals, there is no way you can miss. No go make it happen!

Gloria and Bob Gilstad

"The secret is not how fast you build, but just that you continue to build without quitting."
Gloria Gilstad

Interview conducted with Gloria only.
Background: Real Estate, Business Owner
Year started in networking industry: 1982

Just after we married, when Bob was unemployed, he answered an ad from a network marketing company. At that time, we really needed the opportunity since we were heavily in debt and living on credit. At first we tried the products. Bob used to have migraines and allergies and the products solved those problems. But we also needed a business opportunity to earn an income to survive on.

When I was young, my mother was using products from network marketing companies at wholesale, but she wasn't involved in building her own network. And that was my only exposure to the industry, until Bob answered that ad. We then researched the opportunity and discovered how our work today could be rewarded for years to come.

I was in real estate and Bob used to own a painting business. Eventually we made the leap. I went full-time into network marketing in 1985, while Bob did so in 1987.

My parents were with us 100 percent but most everyone else thought we were crazy. My parents saw the potential it had and made the commitment to work with us. We actually positioned them as our sponsor to make this their retirement. With my education, my sisters thought I should be doing something more "academic." But 15 years later they think we're pretty smart!

I'm not saying we had an easy ride. There were times we had some doubt, too. If things don't move as quickly as you expect, it's easy to think of giving up. A long-term goal keeps you going. Ours was to be financially secure.

And we have exceeded our goals! We've earned over $2 million, and purchased a second home on a lake a few years ago. I think we've proven that network marketing works!

But when we started we had some obstacles. First off, we were broke. We had to borrow money to buy the product and make sure we sold it so we could pay back what we borrowed. Being young was also an obstacle in many ways. Dealing with discouragement, too, was a struggle for us. We had to persevere when things weren't going well. But we kept at it and, in the long-run, we saw the whole picture coming together.

It's very fulfilling to see others succeed. The rewards are great when you can see people accomplish something they never thought they could do. I get just as excited for other people's successes, as I do about my own!

We love working from our home and helping others. Two or three evenings a week we give presentations to prospects. We also travel a lot for business and pleasure, and have gone on 14 travel seminar cruises with our company. We've been to South America, the Caribbean, Mexico, Hawaii, Bermuda, and a dude ranch in Arizona. Last year we went on an African safari to Tanzania. The next trip is to London, England. Our neighbors don't think we have a job. And they're right!

As a sponsor, you can offer the opportunity, training, tools and support, but your distributor needs to supply the motivation. Motivation comes from within. But the sponsor also needs to be a good role model. You can't expect somebody to do something you won't. You also need to support and encourage them and show them you believe they can achieve their dreams. And your being genuinely happy for their success will help build their desire to achieve more.

Bob and I see ourselves as coaches, not managers. There can be drawbacks to managing a downline—it doesn't work. People need to be lead by your example and to feel your support for them. They also need and environment in which to grow, so they can shine by themselves.

We have done just about everything to reach new people including advertising, the Internet, mailings, fairs, trade shows,

fundraisers, and approaching strangers. They all work, but some require more effort than others. Your warm market of friends, business associates, relatives, and acquaintances from school or church can lead to some of your best distributors. We are in the relationship business and these people already have some type of relationship with you that you can build on. What job could you have where you can pick who you want to work with, like you can in network marketing? Maybe the best way to find new distributors is just to make new friends. We have certainly made some wonderful friends in this business!

We need to be careful not to prejudge when talking to new people. Everyone can fit into network marketing when the timing is right. Our philosophy is to share the information and wait until they make the decision it is the right time for them. It can take years for some people to see the opportunity. For example, my sisters weren't interested in the beginning, but now they are.

There are two great ways we use to share our opportunity. One is talking about the products and their benefits first, and then we can get into the business opportunity as their interest grows. The other approach that attracts people is the lifestyle we lead. People have approached *us* because of the freedom and security we have. Being in control of our lives, along with the time flexibility this business offers, gets people's attention.

When someone rejects me, I cry. Just kidding! Rejection is not personal and people aren't rejecting you. People have a right to make their own decisions. There are plenty of people who are looking for what you have to offer; just concentrate on finding the people who want it and not on the people who don't. Always concentrate on the positive—not the rejection.

Thinking fast is an asset in network marketing. This business really gets you out of your comfort zone and stretches you. One time, for example, we had scheduled a big kick-off meeting with the president of our company, and reserved the local bank's community room as the facility. On the night of our big event, we had an amazing challenge dumped into our laps. The bank president had mistakenly taken the community room key with him out of town, and we couldn't get into the room. We quickly had to come up with a back-up plan, so we moved the meeting to the local real estate office.

After moving all of the desks out of the way, and with our guests overflowing the building, we opened the boxes and found the new products had broken their seals in transit. It ended up that our president was in the restroom cleaning the bottles, right up until the point when we introduced him to speak! We learned a lot of things that evening. Always double-check your arrangements and make sure everyone is willing to do whatever it takes to make your event a success!

Consistency is the secret to long-term success. Inactivity is the secret to failure. We all have rejections and discouragement, but don't let that steal your vision away. Find a company you can build your dreams on and give it all your effort. Create a workable business plan for what you want to accomplish, lay your foundation now and put your effort in. You can then see rewards for years and years to come.

Whatever you do, don't think of network marketing as a "get-rich-quick" scheme. Many people quit because they don't understand that this is a very real business that requires hard work and dedication. It's an honest way to build long-term on-going income—by referring people to products you like. The secret is not how fast you build it, but that you continue to build it without quitting.

One quote Bob and I remember from one of the first trainings we attended is, "The only way to fail in network marketing is to quit." If you don't quit, you will succeed.

DREAM ACHIEVERS

FACTOID #3

The top 3 priorities of the Dream Achievers:

63%   God / Family / Business
        in that order

80%   Included Family in top 3

6%   Included Health in top 3

Jim Grande

*"You need to open a lot of oysters
to find the pearls!"*
Jim Grande

Background: Aerospace Industry
Year started in networking industry: 1992

I was not recruited into the industry the way most people are. No one approached me and said they wanted me to see an opportunity. For 18 years I was a rocket scientist for a Fortune 200 aerospace company. It was a decent job and I made six figures. But all of a sudden my wife and I had a child. And although I was very successful, I was working 70 hours a week. So, that's really the reason why I started looking at other opportunities. I was in my mid-30s and wanted to be home with my family.

I researched over 500 different businesses to see what I'd be interested in, including franchises, purchasing, and network marketing. I also set up a list of criteria so I could rate each opportunity. I wanted to choose the right one. After reviewing my criteria, I realized that the concept of on-going income was best for me, so that's what drew me into the industry. It was also important to me that the products were of high quality, filled a niche, and had a recognizable name. I knew this would help us build a residual income with them. One day I responded to an advertisement, and that's when I found the company I'm now with.

My immediate family was very supportive of my decision. But when we started our business, my wife and I didn't tell our friends about it. We had this perception that they would think we were harassing them. We decided to prospect strangers first. That way we could go back to our families and friends later in a position of strength as successful network marketers. But when we finally became very successful, some of our friends and family members actually got mad at us because we hadn't shown them the business early on! So now we advise new network marketers to at least tell their friends and family about the business. After all, it's hard to say who is and who isn't going to be interested in it.

Since I'm very self-confident, I knew having any doubts about the business would hurt us. So, we focused on making it work rather than worrying about it. The biggest surprise I had was finding that some people just didn't do anything. They came into the business wanting to succeed, but for some reason they didn't take action and do the things they needed to do to make it happen. That's when I realized this is a numbers game. The more people I talked to, the more I would find who wouldn't just *say* they wanted to work, but actually did. You need to open a lot of oysters to find the pearls!

A "pearl" is really a self-motivated person. We reach out to as many people as we can and find the ones who are already motivated. Once we find them, we ask what they want out of life and then we show them how they can use our company's business opportunity to get it. Helping people achieve a better life and seeing them accomplish it motivates me. I like sharing excitement! And since I've been on the cover of *Success* magazine, people listen!

I believe that building a network marketing business involves a sifting process. The main thing is to keep looking for the people who want to build a business, and if some people say no along the way, that's perfectly fine. I've discovered I really have no idea who is going to become successful. I don't prejudge anyone. For example, I have a distant relative who joined my company. And since he was so low-key, we didn't think he'd be successful. But the great thing is this guy's approach. He says, "If I can do it, you can do it," and he has become the most successful person in our downline!

Another time we had a lady call us up and say, "I know about your company's product line. You have one product that I think is unbelievable, but the rest of them stink!" The product she was talking about is great for diaper rash. In fact, she went on to say it was so great that she could sell 30 cans of this stuff just by telling people. She just raved about it. So I asked her what she thought about our other 349 products and she said she hadn't tried any of them. I started laughing and when she asked why, I said, "Well, I'd love to see what's going to happen when you try those products as well!" She was a motivated person, but she didn't see the opportunity until I pointed it out to her.

The best thing about network marketing is that we don't wake up to an alarm clock anymore. I know that sounds trivial, but when you never have to wake up to a loud buzzing sound again, it gives you a great feeling. I wake up when my body says it's time! I work out in the morning and after that I spend time with my son. Children are creative, especially in the morning. So, my mornings are spent with him as a "special time" for me. After that I either go to a coffee shop or the beach to plan my day. I figure out who I'm going to approach with my business opportunity and how I'll approach them. And then I meet with people.

Most of our conversations are on the phone, but I meet with a lot of my leaders at the beach and spend time with them. We have built great relationships and that's something we're very happy about.

There really is no typical day, but the priorities are the same each day—talk to new people, keep in contact with the leaders who are already working the business with me, and spend the rest of the day with my family. George Burns once said, "Find something you love and you'll never work a day in your life." I love that quote because that's how I feel about network marketing.

To build a strong network marketing business, there must be a strong sense of "why." A person must have a strong desire to succeed. They also need to have a sense of urgency and persist. I can almost guarantee someone that if they never quit, they will succeed. There are all kinds of bumps and hurdles along the way, but if you never quit, it will work eventually. The last key is passion. You need to be passionate about the products and the opportunity.

Perhaps a main reason why people quit network marketing is because the new person hasn't made a connection between what they want and how to get it. They may have read somewhere that they can make a million dollars in network marketing, but they're not sure of the exact steps.

To alleviate that problem, determine what you really want. What's your dream? Then make the commitment to make it happen and take action. Sit down and develop a plan. Get in touch with your sponsor and ask for help. Most importantly, realize that you are the only one standing in the way of your success.

Mary Griffin

"I love working out of my home!"
Mary Griffin

Background: Teaching
Year started in networking industry: 1988

When I first got started in network marketing, I had no home or car. I was living in my friend's basement with my eight-year-old daughter, surviving on food stamps. I can tell you now, from someone who's been on both sides of the fence, *network marketing works!*

I was a Girl Scout leader and at one of the meetings a new mother approached me with a network marketing opportunity. I'm a trained elementary school teacher and was home-schooling my daughter at the time, so the idea of a home-based business appealed to me.

At first I was only interested in the products that this woman was selling. But when she explained the business opportunity to me, I thought, "Wow! You can really make some money here!" That's when I signed up.

No one was supportive of my decision to get into network marketing. My mother thought I was "wasting my education" and everyone else thought I'd just end up wasting my time. But I was in such a bad financial bind that I pretty much decided I didn't care what anyone else thought—and that I was going to succeed with or without them!

The pain of watching the tears in my daughter's eyes when we had to leave our farm in Colorado left me heartbroken. I had owned that home for twelve years and I was determined to provide a better life for her. I just knew that network marketing was eventually going to make everything okay.

My mom let me borrow her jalopy car and off I went to make my business explode! I thought my friends and family would join the business with me. I was sure surprised when they showed no interest. That was a hard lesson to learn. So, I went beyond my circle of influence and talked to everybody, everybody, and everybody else!

The company I'm with now isn't the first company I joined. In that first company, however, I am proud to say that I became the first single mother to become one of the top ten distributors in the nation. I won several cruise trips and a few cars, and I was finally proving to everyone that network marketing worked.

I eventually discovered a product line that really "wowed" me. My company has a wonderful whole-food product line that I immediately fell in love with. They are highly nutritious and with the exception of water, you can literally eat nothing else and live on these products. They contain real foods such as nuts, grains, fruits and seeds, and supply your body with everything it needs to function optimally. Considering what the standard American diet consisted of, I thought that everyone could use these products!

The products truly motivated me to succeed because they were highly nutritious and could help a lot of people.

Network marketing gives you the power to help people gain control over their financial situations. I love watching people I've brought into the business win trips and awards. Knowing I played a part in their success gives meaning to what I do. My network marketing business isn't valuable to me only in terms of money, but also in terms of humanity. With my opportunity, I can help so many improve their lives.

My mom is a great example. She is 79 years old and I was able to help build an organization under her. She earns ongoing income every month and I really don't know how she would have survived without it.

I love working out of my home! I never want to drive to work again in rush hour, work for someone else for eight hours, and then drive back home in rush hour. My time is *my* time now, and I love it! After I get my family off to work and school early in the morning, I exercise. Then I put on my telephone headset and talk all day! I can do the dishes, laundry, whatever, while still talking to people—sharing our company and products.

I do three-way and conference calls, and then set aside time to prepare and send out information packets and product samples.

When I first started working my business, I put in 12 hours a day, seven days a week. But I knew that a successful network marketing organization gains momentum over time. So, when my commission checks started growing consistently, I cut back on my hours. That's the beauty of this business. And I am my own boss!

I find that meetings are only worthwhile when they're meaningful. When I introduce somebody to the industry of network marketing, I do it over the phone. I don't see the benefit of inviting a person to a meeting to learn about your opportunity when you can just as easily call them up and give them the same information.

However, a meeting that is held for the purpose of recognizing distributors for their successes is essential. I am a big believer in applauding and awarding people for working hard and achieving their goals.

Training meetings are also important. These meetings focus on the how and why of the business and we get as many new distributors as possible plugged into them.

The people who are new to network marketing seem to make the best business partners. They haven't been discouraged by previous opportunities and they are excited. Once I see that enthusiasm, I work with them closely. I know if I help them succeed as quickly as possible that will generate even more excitement.

It's important to talk to everybody when recruiting because you never know who you'll stumble across. Yes, I follow the three-foot rule; I talk to everyone within three feet of me about network marketing!

When I approach someone with my opportunity, I ask them about their goals and dreams. They need to tell me what they want to achieve. Then I can share with them how my company's business opportunity will help them get it. I need to hear their why.

Once I hear them say "I want to make more money" or "I want more time freedom," then I immediately show them how I can help.

Asking someone about their goals and dreams is personal, and some people may think it's not necessary to get personal with a new prospect to build a business. But network marketing is a business built on relationships and being real with people. And how else can you build a relationship if you *don't* ask them about their goals and dreams?

You need to get personal with people in order to strike a chord in them. I'll tell you a story that basically sums up why being real is so important.

My company was holding a training meeting and I was asked to be one of the speakers. Hundreds of people attended this meeting and I was very excited about sharing my experiences with them. When I arrived for the engagement, a sound technician clipped a wireless microphone on me, but what I didn't know was that the sound was turned on long before the meeting began. There was some time before I spoke, so I went into the bathroom and relieved myself. I also had conversations with people and all the while my microphone was on!

I was finally told what was happening, but I still went out on stage to speak. I was extremely embarrassed because these people were looking at me as a mentor, yet there I was, this big income earner who everyone just heard in the bathroom! So, when I started my talk I jokingly said, "See? I'm just as human as you are!" We all had a laugh!

My candid statement about being just as human as they are probably meant more to them than anything else I could have said. They realized my success wasn't a result of my being special or having an ability they didn't. I was just a real human being with a desire to succeed. I believe I struck a chord with them that day.

If you want to succeed in network marketing, find the thing that's going to motivate you. If you don't, two things will happen. First, no one in your upline will work with you. The seasoned network marketer knows that those who don't have their why in place won't stay motivated. That, of course, means they'll lose interest, and we all know what happens after that!

The second thing is you will never find yourself fully committed to making your dreams come true. Achieving all the things you want in life comes down to being committed to doing what it takes to achieve them. If you're not fully committed to network marketing, you won't ever get the results you're looking for.

There is no ceiling on your income potential in network marketing. You really can make all the money you want, but you need to remember, it's called net-*working*, not net-*sitting!* It amuses me how so many people get involved, do nothing, and then complain it's not working.

If you ever think it's not working, reevaluate your efforts. Have you set unrealistic goals for yourself? Are you expecting too much too soon? Are you putting in enough hours? More importantly, have you chosen the right company in the first place?

After you iron out your work habits and find a mentor, learn as much as you can and be persistent. When I first started in this industry, my check was $21 a month. Six months later it was only up to $50 a month! Today I'm making my dreams come true. If I had quit back when my check was only $50, I wouldn't be where I am now!

Chuck and Sandra Hoover

"I want my great, great grandchildren to look at a picture of me on the wall and say, 'That's the man who started this thing.'"
Chuck Hoover

Interview conducted with Chuck only.
Background: Business Owner, Construction, Sales
Year started in networking industry: 1987

Before network marketing, I sold automobiles for 20 years. I owned a finance company and an auto dealership for some time. I was also into construction for a while. Then one day a gentleman who worked for me told me he had his own business on the side. When I found out he was doing something extra I told him I was open-minded and interested in hearing about his business. When I discovered network marketing, I saw my life change before my eyes.

Looking back, I don't think I ever had doubts as to whether or not I would be successful. I was just searching for the right vehicle. I would drive through the affluent neighborhoods and look at all the luxury homes. I knew nobody could be more dedicated to becoming successful than me, and I wondered how I could do it. I was looking for the right thing that would fit me. When my company came along, I realized I had found it.

I felt long distance rates and network marketing was a good combination. I had gone through the oil crunch and the banks were affected. Real estate and gas were up and down, but the long distance industry had never been down!

I just wanted to be successful. Success, to me, is living every day the way I want to live it. If I want to get up in the morning and fly to San Francisco and eat breakfast, it is *my* choice. Being the master of my own destiny was a driving force. I also don't want to be buried without an epitaph. I want to make a difference! I want my great, great grandchildren to look at a picture of me on the wall and say, "That's the man who started this thing." I want them to be distributors and work the business they way I did. Network marketing has made a serious difference in my life and the lives of my family members. For instance, I enjoy going to lunch with my grandchildren in grade school!

My family and friends have always respected my business decisions, so they supported me 100 percent. I worked with a lot of strangers in the beginning because the majority of my warm market already wanted in!

But it was frustrating to grapple with the fact that I wanted people to have success more than they wanted it for themselves. I had to realize that some people were going to do it, while others weren't. I couldn't force anyone to do this. I kept searching for people who wanted to change their lives. And I've realized they're everywhere.

In fact, my best reps have come out of desperation. They come to a point in life where they need a change and are looking for the right opportunity. Age, race, gender, and education have nothing to do with it. Desire is where it's at. People who are ready for a change are the best reps.

When I approach people, mostly I talk about them and not about my business. Two things build the business: excitement and money. I also listen more than anything else. If I'm sitting at the airport having a conversation, something is eventually going to give me a door opener like, "Man, I never get time for a vacation!" I will say, "You might want to take a look at what I'm doing." I get their card and tell them I will get back to them.

I am not ashamed of what I do. In fact, I'm very proud and excited about it. If people say to me, "You can do it because of your personality," I say, "If I can do it, you can too." I also answer a question with a question. Somebody once asked Johnny Carson why he always answers a question with a question, and his response was, "Do I do that?" If someone says, "Is that network marketing?" I say, "Do you like network marketing?" By answering questions with questions, you are always listening!

Rejection doesn't bother me at all. Conceptually, if you are only looking for people who want to change their lives, there

can be no rejection. Otherwise it's a timing thing. The time might not be right for those who say no. The only thing constant in life is change. People change and need or want this opportunity at different times. They either want it or they don't. That's why there are so many different products on the market! Some people want a certain brand of soda and others don't. It's not rejection; it's just selection!

My job is to put my new business partners on the road to fulfilling their dreams. I get excited by sharing the knowledge I've gained to help keep them from making mistakes. When people tell me they're sending their kids to college when they never thought they could afford it, or when they buy their first home, there is no better feeling.

On a typical day, my wife and I wake up around 7:30 a.m. to make phone calls until about 11 a.m. We call people in our organization throughout the country. Then I hit the road and do a luncheon, get ready for a meeting, or go prospecting. I typically prospect by meeting people somewhere nice—a financial center, a gallery, or a restaurant—anywhere a conversation can start. Always have your antenna out.

Once a month I have a commitment meeting with my leaders at my home. We discuss our business plans, goals, and time frames to achieve them. And we do that as a team. Network marketing is a team effort, not an individual one. I learned in the military that you can't work with hundreds of people at the same time, but you can work with five who can whip hundreds into shape. So I work with five key people at a time.

We also hold weekly meetings because I believe the sheep that strays gets sheared! On Tuesday nights we have a meeting where 100 to 150 people attend. On Wednesdays I go to meetings of about 50 people, and on Thursdays it's another 100 people or so. On Fridays we have a small meeting where one of my leaders runs it, so I can spend personal time with their organization.

I also travel about once a month to corporate events throughout the country, where about 500 to 2000 people attend. Then, once a year we have a national meeting in Dallas and about 12,000 to 15,000 people are there from all over the country. I spend about 80 hours a week running my business. But I love what I do! I am not a ten-hour-a-week person.

I believe that leadership, above all, is the heartbeat of any successful organization. A leader is a director who shows you what can be achieved by proving it can be done. A leader also helps you achieve your dreams. For example, if I know you are going someplace, I will help you get there faster by getting in your boat and paddling with you. People tend more to do what you do, rather than what you say to do. If I don't have a guest at the meeting, how are you going to have one?

I am a firm believer in doing whatever it takes to become successful. They always say that successful people do the things unsuccessful people don't. For example, early on in my business I was in St. Louis and out of money. All I could afford was the meeting room. So, every day I changed and shaved in the bathroom and slept on the chaise lounge by the pool. One night a security guard came up and said I couldn't sleep there. I replied, "I am not spending another night with that woman. You understand me?" He said, "I understand" and left me alone!

Of course, I was joking. But I did whatever it took to make my business work. I wasn't wealthy when I started so I can really relate to most everybody who starts in this industry. I think that one of the reasons why I appreciate what I do today is because I came from nothing and built it from scratch.

I think a lot of people quit network marketing because they're used to quitting. It's a sad fact, but so many people somehow want to blame their failures on everyone else. They'll write you letters and tell you why they're quitting and it's always someone else's fault: "My sponsor didn't give me any help," "The company lost my customer," or "I didn't receive my kit in time." No one ever wrote me a letter that said, "Chuck, I'm quitting network marketing because that's just what I do. I have quit a lot of things in the past and I'm looking forward to quitting a lot of things in the future, and right now I'm quitting network marketing." They don't take responsibility. That's why I am always looking for people who want to make a change in their lives.

The key to success is to believe in yourself and your abilities. Quitting is never an option for me. I heard once that Walt Disney claimed bankruptcy seven times. No matter what happened, he never quit on his dreams. If you believe success will happen for you, it will.

For anyone getting involved in network marketing for the first time, the more excited you are the better. Take advantage of that excitement and talk to as many people as possible. Enthusiasm can generate a mountain of interest! But don't just sell people into the business. Instead, find people who are just as enthusiastic about changing their lives as you are.

Also, if you don't know the answer to something, it's okay to admit it and say "I don't know." Teach your reps that they can build their businesses only by signing up customers and recruiting people to do the same thing. Anything else they do is just excess baggage! Could A.J. Foyt (champion race car driver) have ever won a race if he was just towing his car? Leave all the garbage behind and do what you get paid for.

Winners keep doing it and doing it—until it works. So do it and be a winner!

Dave and Valerie Johnson

*"Life is so exciting when
you have a dream!"*
Dave Johnson

Interview conducted with Dave only.
Background: Sales, Military
Year started in networking industry: 1976

O ne day, after I got married, I found myself wondering,
"What do I want to do when I grow up?" Before network
marketing I had many different jobs including dishwasher,
forklift operator, landscaper, light bulb salesman, electronic technician,
and Coca Cola bottle sorter. Perhaps the best example of my "clear"
career focus is my personal record of five W-2 (employee wage statement) forms in one year!

I entered Navy boot camp when I was 24 years old as a way to
get ahead. I had joined the Navy to pursue a career in electronics.
Two years later I had had enough of electronics! I was then 26, and
I still had no idea of what path I wanted to take.

Around this time a friend invited my wife and me over to his
house for what I thought would be just a visit. This invitation turned
out to be for a presentation on network marketing. What I learned at
that little home meeting changed my whole life! My mind was
opened to tremendous possibilities and the vision of really doing
something wonderful with my life. Life is so exciting when you
have a dream!

**Life is a "do-it-yourself project." This was one of the great
revelations of network marketing for me.** I had always been willing
to work hard. But now it was different because I had a plan. Network
marketing became my road map. I had hold of a powerful vehicle and
I could change my whole life by changing my thoughts and actions.

**Where you will be in the future depends upon the books you
read, the tapes you listen to, and the people you associate with.** I

began to hang around the people in my company that were doing something. I read good books, listened to tapes, and went to work!

The first several network marketing companies I joined gave me tremendous experience, but not a lot of financial success. In a way they taught me how to drive—I just didn't have the right vehicle! I had learned a lot in my 14 years of network marketing. However, I was still broke!

Sometimes being broke would get me a little discouraged and I would think, "If network marketing is supposed to be so good, then why isn't it happening for me?" But I kept reminding myself that I was heading in the right direction, and that I was learning and growing.

The company I'm with now is my fourth. And since I'm now successful, this proves that persistence pays off. When I saw this particular opportunity, I knew I could make it work and I just had to be a part of it. And with all of my previous experience, I was well prepared!

In our first year with this company, my wife and I made $200,000. It was almost scary how quickly we were succeeding! I gave so many years of my life to so many different jobs, yet none of them compensated me in the way that network marketing has. Nothing before ever gave me the opportunity to put myself in a position that truly helped people.

Anyone with an attractive personality, a caring heart, and a strong work ethic can make lots of new friends. They can also build an empire and positively change the lives of thousands of people when they do whatever it takes to make it happen.

I have heard it said that "If you want something and don't get it, you either didn't really want it or you tried to bargain over the price." H.L. Hunt said the key to success is as follows: 1. Decide what you want; 2. Be willing to pay the price; and 3. Get to work. If you really want to build a successful network marketing business, please give yourself some time to figure it out. Once you have the skills, always remember that it will probably take three to five years to succeed.

All I wanted to do with my network marketing company was make a difference. I wanted my life to have a purpose. And helping people change and improve their lives is what drives me to succeed every day.

I heard a quote once that sums it up for me. It goes, "Happy is the man who has found his worship, wife and work, and loves all three." Aside from that, what else in life really matters?

I have greatly enjoyed the time freedom network marketing has given me, and I've recently become obsessed with the piano! I've got a nine-and-a-half-foot Bosendorfer piano being delivered soon. And I even fly out of state once a month to take lessons from a professor. The time freedom my family and I have now is precious. And because of that, we have taken trips to Hawaii, Jamaica, Scandinavia, and DisneyWorld, as well as ski trips and cruises.

There's a misconception that you can't motivate anyone but yourself. I don't think that's an accurate statement. I've certainly been motivated! And I consider motivating and inspiring people as part of my job.

One of the best ways I motivate people is to help them find a new, *excited* distributor in their downline and work with them. That usually wakes the non-motivated distributor right up! And I love to light fires under people!

Most people complain about one of two things: they either don't have enough money or they don't have enough time. But in network marketing, when you're committed to your opportunity and take appropriate action, you can eventually have enough of both. When I approach people with my opportunity, I know they'll complain about the lack of one or the other. I listen to find out which one they want, and then show them how network marketing can help them get it. I basically let the products and opportunity speak for themselves and leave the decision up to the prospect.

If a person rejects my offer to help them improve their life, I accept their rejection. When you call up your friend and ask them to come over for a piece of pie, and they say no, you wouldn't lie awake in bed all night pining over their refusal, would you? Of course not! So why get upset if your friend refuses your business opportunity? Network marketing is a numbers game and the fact that some people aren't ready is just fine.

There are times when a distributor calls to tell me they're quitting the industry, and I say, "How can you quit? You never got started!" They'll rationalize that the industry isn't right for them and all they did was call their best friend who refused them. It's sad that some people can't treat small obstacles as growth challenges rather than roadblocks. The fact is there are no easy, high-paying jobs, yet so many people are on a quest to find them.

To succeed in network marketing, find a mentor and duplicate what they do. Listen to how they talk to prospects on the phone and watch how they approach people. You will learn so much by observing those who are already succeeding.

Also, if you have any hang-ups or insecurities, get rid of them! You will fail if you don't change the negative behaviors and beliefs that have held you back for so long. Network marketing is a wonderful course in psychology and human relations, and doing some heavy-duty analysis on yourself will help you better understand other people.

Perhaps the most important key to success is duplication. A simple, duplicatable system is the backbone of a successful network marketing business. When you bring people into your organization, be sure to teach them everything you know about network marketing. Then teach them to teach their organizations, and so on.

There's a fantastic quote by Rudyard Kipling that says, "The great focal point in life is when opportunity and preparedness meet." If you are ready to finally succeed in life and you have found a company and a product line that you can be excited about, then go after your dreams. *Make a decision!*

Don't even think about getting involved if you won't make at least a one-year, all-out commitment. Follow your heart and find a company that really puts some fire in your belly. Then let your passion drive you!

Hans and Danette Johnson

*"People will work harder for
recognition than anything else."*
Hans and Danette Johnson

Background: Underwater Construction Diver
Year started in networking industry:
Hans 1991, Danette 1989

Q: What did you do before network marketing?
Danette: We were teenagers! Hans was 18 and I was 19. I was on my own since age 16, and changed jobs 13 times in five years.
Hans: I was working as a commercial diver doing underwater construction for about 60 hours a week.

Q: How did you get introduced to network marketing?
Hans: A high school friend bumped into me at a local gym and he told me he had just made $700 in about three hours. He then invited me to a business presentation, where Danette was speaking. That's how we met. So I was sold twice that day!
Danette: I was introduced by a friend who was very persistent with me for three months until I finally went to a presentation.

Q: Were your family and friends supportive of your decision to start a network marketing business?
Hans: Not at all! I quit my job and moved out to California. They thought I was brainwashed.
Danette: I didn't have too many friends. I was a loner in high school, and I moved out of my hometown when I was 18. I didn't know anybody when I began this business.

Q: Did you ever have self-doubt?
Danette: Absolutely. It took me three months before I got in because I thought it was too good to be true. But once I understood it, I bought it hook, line, and sinker. In nine years, my worst year in

earnings was $70,000. My belief in myself was very high because I saw other people making good money and I knew I could do it too.

Hans: I always wanted to be an entrepreneur. I grew up in a family that didn't have a lot of money and had to use food stamps. Danette and I worked for a long time putting in 18-hour days to make the business work. We believed we had to sacrifice in the beginning to achieve long-term financial success.

Q: How did the quality of the products influence your decision to join?

Hans: Not a bit! But it so happens that the products are awesome. Many people working this opportunity don't have sales experience but that doesn't matter. The products are so good that they can't keep them on hand.

Q: What was your driving motivation to succeed in your new business?

Danette: I wanted to provide for my family and not have to survive on welfare. Because of what Hans and I went through to get here, we have 100 percent passion and belief in ourselves, the company and what it can do for people.

Hans: When I was young, my brother and I sometimes had to pick flowers and sell them so we could eat dinner. I didn't want that to happen when I had a family. I wanted to properly provide for them. So our main passion today is centered on our family.

Q: Describe a typical day/week.

Danette: I work 16 to 20 hours a week. During a typical day I am scheduling appointments. I don't do any shortcuts like advertising and major marketing stuff. Eighty percent of my time is spent sitting in front of a live body sharing our business opportunity. About 20 percent of my time is spent training people I get into the business. We do a three-meeting plan with everyone we sponsor. The first meeting is the business presentation. When they join up, I contact them within 24 to 48 hours and do training over the phone. Then 24 to 48 hours after training them, we're in their living room helping them make money.

Hans: I work an average of 20 hours a week, primarily with new distributors. I help them get started and set up their business as a real business. I do trainings and help them arrange their schedules, meetings and phone calls. I also talk to them about goal-setting.

Q: Do you use meetings and events to grow your business?
Danette: Yes, that's how our business grows! We have a co-op where everyone meets every Tuesday and Saturday. There are three areas to our business: expose, involve, and upgrade. Hans and I do that every day.

Q: Describe how you motivate your downline.
Hans: We have monthly trainings that run for an entire weekend. They're two-day workshops where our distributors are totally focused on learning all they can to make their businesses explode. We've had a lot of great success with people leaving the training and making $20,000 to $100,000 their first year working just 10 to 20 hours a week.
Danette: We also have a voicemail system that allows us to send out hundreds of motivational messages to our downline—training, recognition, update, and informational messages.
Hans: Our company is very big on recognition. We feel it helps keep people in long enough to succeed. People will work harder for recognition than anything else.

Q: What value do you place on managing your downline?
Danette: We don't worry about managing. This is a recruiting business—a numbers game. Managing won't help us here!
Hans: The only way to grow your business is through recruiting. Through proper leadership you can maintain what you have. Some people focus only on recruiting but not maintaining. There is a delicate balance needed there and that is why we have the training seminars.

Q: How do you deal with rejection?
Hans: Two things. First, you need to have a "Who cares?" attitude. The second thing is to reject them first! If there are people you know who just won't do it, tell them they can't do it and it's not for them. Of course you want to be professional and polite. The only reason why someone won't start in the business is because of timing. Maybe now is not the right time but when their job goes bad in

a few months it might be the perfect time. You follow up with them periodically. Don't wait for them, and keep sorting.

Q: Is everyone a potential recruit for you?
Danette: Everyone is a potential recruit; however, I am not going to waste a lot of time begging anyone to do this. I am looking for leaders. But, even if they are not great leaders, they can lead us to people who will help their businesses grow.

Q: What is your most effective approach when talking to people about your business?
Danette: I wear a button. It says "I am excited, ask me why" or, "I have a new attitude, ask me why." I have worn a button for seven years and a major part of our organization came from positive responses to the buttons! When people ask me about it I say, "I work with a company that offers a home-based business opportunity. It has helped me and my husband. What do you do?"

From there I build rapport, get their number, follow up with a phone call, and do the presentation. Twenty-four hours later I am training them and 24 hours after that I'm in their home! That's the process! The other thing we do is prepare them for rejection. We tell them that their friends and family are not all going to be excited about this. But if they weather the storm, they will eventually join and be supportive or somehow involved. We sell them a promise to the future.

Q: How do you do your presentations?
Danette: We do a whiteboard presentation for groups and use a sheet of paper for our sit-downs. We ask a lot of questions that build a want. For groups we ask these questions: "If money were no object, how would your life look?" "How many of you would live in a different house?" "How many would drive a different car?" And "How many of you would have a healthy retirement set up?" Then we ask, "If you continue on the path you're on now, will you ever be able to achieve all those things?" Ninety-nine percent of the people in the room say no. I then ask, "Are you willing *not* to have all those things?"

The next question I ask is: "Would you be willing to work, learn, and try something for the next five years of your life for five to ten hours a week, to have all those things you said you wanted and more?" All the hands in the room go up! Then we show them how to start.

Q: Why do you think people quit network marketing?
Danette: There are five types of distributors. First is the "Product User." If you recognize them for using the product, they will never go away. Second is the "Social Distributor." If you recognize them for being part of something great and introduce them to other people, they will never go away. Third is the "Seasonal Distributor." This person makes a ton of money quick to pay bills and then disappears for a little while. When he does return, you make him feel welcome so he will come back again when he has another goal to reach. Fourth is the "Part-Time Distributor." This person wants to make some extra money every month. If you recognize him or her for selling a few hundred dollars worth of product a month, he or she will continue to do it. Last is the "All Out Blaster." This person wants to be a superstar! When you recognize people for who they are, your attrition will be really low.

Q: What advice could you give to people who are just starting out in network marketing?
Hans: You need to have the right company with consumable products that both affect people emotionally and are replaced on a monthly basis. Make sure you are working with the right team with proven experience. The right intentions without experience will go nowhere. The right experience with right intentions is a gold mine! If I needed brain surgery, I wouldn't want a studying M.D. doing his or her residency and internship to perform something he or she knows little about. I would want a brain surgeon who's performed this many times.

You also need a compensation plan that rewards everyone, from the person who wants to earn $100 a month to the person who wants to earn $100,000 or more their first year working part-time. The compensation plan also needs to have lots of recognition programs. Have a good training system and keep your priorities straight. Find someone who is successful, model them, and never ever quit!

Tony Kent

*"The quality of our lives
is determined by the quality of
our decisions."*
Tony Kent

Background: Fashion Industry
Year started in networking industry: 1986

Before network marketing, I lived in Europe for 25 years
as a fashion photographer. I photographed hundreds of
famous people including Presidents Nixon and Francois
Mitterand, Grace Kelly and the Royal Family of Monaco, the Rolling Stones, Catherine Deneuve, Yves Montand, Gene Hackman,
Audrey Hepburn, Carl Lewis, and Raquel Welch, to name just a
few. I've traveled the world all my life and I've had some really
great experiences. But that made it hard for me to spend time with
my four children. They were growing up so fast and I wanted to be
there for them more than I was. So I started looking for a business
that I could run from home, and that's when I found network marketing.

I saw an ad in a newspaper and went to a hotel meeting for a
brand new network marketing company. What got me interested in
joining was the concept of residual income. I knew what residual
income was because of some of the celebrities I worked with.
When I photographed the Rolling Stones, I came to understand
that just one of their albums would continually generate income
long after the work was done on it, and that concept has always
fascinated me.

**Over the next few years I tried a variety of different network
marketing companies.** I wanted to find the perfect company for
me. During that time my wife and I ended a relationship after 25
years and I found myself a single parent of four kids! I was going
through a lot and my self-esteem was at an all-time low. But I
found the strength to channel all that pain into the passion to suc-

ceed, and I started doing extremely well in the network marketing company that I was involved in.

What eventually attracted me to the company I'm with now was their business strategy and humanitarian vision. I fully believe in the concept of using the Internet to generate income. And they were the only Internet company I saw that embraced network marketing and had an Internet strategy rather than just an Internet presence. The potential really excited me! I was also very impressed with the founders' mission of building an Internet community that would "help the little guy, and return a significant portion of their success to charitable contributions and to communities."

To me, a major essence of network marketing is realizing that opportunity is everywhere. When I saw the presentation and talked with the founders, I was convinced. I had finally discovered the opportunity that meshed with my beliefs. And I felt it had everything in place for them to be a world-class company that fully embraced network marketing.

Network marketing is sharing something you really love with people you care about. Our company is known as "The world's most valued online community." I like knowing that, by getting people involved in the opportunity, I'm adding value to their lives. Because of my efforts, so many people have the chance to create richer, more meaningful lives. This industry has given me such a great sense of purpose!

In my heart I hold a passion to help people help themselves. I know that if I go out and do everything each day with integrity, truth, passion and love in my heart, I will succeed. But what I love even more is that I will be helping *other people* succeed.

What I teach my distributors to do is duplicate a program we use called "The Science to Success." This system teaches people how to find three business partners and five customers, and then go out and duplicate that same process. Everyone wants to be a part of a high performance team. Our system really stresses this and it allows people to truly experience what it is like to have a mentor and be on a team, which I feel are two of the major keys to being successful in our industry. This is part of the core of my business philosophy.

I work every day, seven days a week, and I actually enjoy the workload because I am so thankful to have this great opportunity. I spend a lot of time on the phone; sometimes all day and a lot of the night! My time is spent talking to people about having more in life, building relationships, and conquering challenges. I believe that everyone can make it in network marketing, but most people need help and guidance and partners to work with them.

On weekends, I am available for trainings, three-way calls and one-on-one presentations, or whatever my team asks of me. One of my biggest passions is my children, so I always make sure I am available whenever they need me. Balancing family life and business during the building of an organization is a very valued skill set, and I encourage everyone to pay a lot of attention to their family at all times.

A lot of people have never met anyone who actually does network marketing, so it's nice to show people an alternate way to make a living! And when they hear about my success, it reassures them that it really can be done. Success in network marketing isn't just a rumor.

When motivating my downline, I love to help people open up and trust their greatness. We all have vast, unlimited power to draw on but, until you realize it, it won't do you any good. Every person has something very special about them, and I believe that network marketing is a great platform for people to be able to showcase their talents and abilities and make a contribution with their lives.

There's an old adage that says there are two ways to fail in network marketing: don't start or quit. Some people forget that it's called net-*work* marketing! They forget to work!

People ask me how to deal with rejection and all I can say is I don't. I simply accept the fact that the person I'm talking to doesn't see the value in becoming a part of the network marketing community. That's just the way it is!

I always present my information in a way that gives my prospect a full understanding of what I have to offer. This way, when they say no, they're saying an educated no, not an ignorant no. I never want anyone to say no because they don't understand my opportunity, so I'm always conveying my information in the best way I can.

If a person quits network marketing, it is usually that they're not passionate about what they're doing. They soon realize that what they want is to make a quick buck, and that's not what happens in this industry. A person can join a network marketing company, work full-out for three months, and still not make much money. The way income is generated in network marketing is indeed different than the traditional "dollars-for-hours" method that most people are familiar with.

The fact is, you are severely underpaid for your hard work when you first start out. That's one of the greatest challenges of network marketing, but it's also true for most new business start-ups. However, unlike most conventional businesses, once you get past that low-income period you will see that, as time goes on, you can work less and less while generating more and more income. That is the beauty of network marketing! Unfortunately, many people may not understand that their income starts at zero, and it takes time for them to grow themselves and their businesses. Instead, they often have the idea that network marketing is a get-rich-quick deal—which couldn't be further from the truth. I want people to know that they need to grow personally because no one can build an organization bigger than they are. So, on our team, we stress personal growth at all times.

People also quit because of lack of support from their upline. As a network marketing business owner, it is imperative to be a leader for your organization. If you stop helping them, how can you succeed? Remember that your income derives from a percentage of the success you help others attain. Again, you need to be passionate about helping people reach their goals if you want to make it in this industry.

What it all boils down to is love and passion. Love is what gives life to everything, and passion creates all-out massive action. When I endeavor to enroll a new prospect, I ask them what they're passionate about, what their goal in life is. Then I ask if they have a plan or a vehicle to reach that goal. If they say no, I tell them about my business opportunity and share with them how this can be the vehicle that may allow them to live their dreams.

If you are looking for a network marketing opportunity, find the company that makes you vibrate! Fall in love with the company's philosophy and products and then honestly acknowledge how much you want to succeed.

Remember, it's not the income you make that matters. It's how much of a contribution you can make to society that will fill you up and catapult you into success.

What is your "purpose"? If you ask the average person what their purpose is, they won't be able to tell you. One of my favorite books is *The Path* by Laurie Beth Jones. She says that everyone should be able to define their purpose in ten words or less, so that even a ten-year-old can understand you.

The reason for defining your purpose is to come up with a personal mission. This way, when you're faced with a decision or problem, you can easily deal with it because it either fits or doesn't fit into your mission. In every moment you have a choice, and every choice is part of your destiny. However, the quality of our lives is determined by the quality of our decisions.

So, define your purpose and find goals that are in alignment with it. Once you start examining what you really want in life, you'll find a whole new world!

Carl Jung, who was one of the world's greatest psychiatrists, once said, "Nothing so much affects the life of a child than a parent's unfulfilled life." I'll tell you, that continues to be a major motivator for me. When I die, I want my children to know that I followed my heart, and that I strived to make every moment of my existence meaningful and adventurous.

If you don't live your dream, you're going to end up living somebody else's! See the bigger picture. See outside that "I have a J-O-B and work for someone else" box that most people live in. See your options! See the power you possess, and the time freedom you can have with network marketing.

Understand that, even though you are just one person, you have the ability to help hundreds of thousands of other people enrich their lives with your opportunity. In so doing, you get to make a difference with and in *your* life!

Shane D. Klippenes

"Confidence breeds competence!"
Shane D. Klippenes

Background: Food Service
Year started in networking industry: 1995

Before network marketing, I was a grocery store manager. It wasn't the greatest job, but I'm a hard worker so I made pretty good money. I was also a college student and banged up my knee playing hockey.

My wife's father was a network marketing distributor and had a liquid mineral product which he thought would help my injury. I was skeptical at first, but not long after taking the product the pain in my knee was completely gone and I was very impressed. That's when I took a look at the business side of his opportunity.

I eventually decided to go into network marketing full time. When I announced to everyone that I was quitting my grocery store job I certainly raised a few eyebrows. But today, now that I'm doing very well, I have a lot of enthusiastic support.

I did doubt myself right after I quit my job, though. I had to get over a lot of the horror stories I heard about the industry. But I kept focusing on the good things that I could accomplish with my opportunity and that kept me on track.

When I developed a total belief in our products and opportunity, I made the transition from the attitude of an employee to the attitude of a business owner. Once I made that change, self-doubt became a thing of the past. Also, I feel good selling a product that millions of people really need. I became a distributor to share a product that would make an exponential difference in hundreds of thousands of people's lives. If our product line was something I didn't believe in, I couldn't have succeeded.

The most fulfilling thing that has come out of network marketing for me is having the time and financial freedom to be able to have my wife be a stay-at-home mom, and to be there myself for a lot of the neat moments our girls have. Taking my wife to lunch or playing with my girls at the pool on a weekday, while other fathers are working, is priceless. Spending time with my family is my ultimate reward for a job well done in network marketing. And anyone with clear goals and enough desire to get there can do it.

Being able to help other people realize dramatic improvements in their health and lifestyles is also a source of great fulfillment and a driving force for me. For example, we had a woman with chronic fatigue syndrome come into our office a while ago. She said that by 3 p.m. she had to lie down, was done in for the rest of the evening and slept for hours. She started on our products and came back a few weeks later in tears. She looked at my father-in-law and me and said, "You guys gave me my life back." She then told us that she wasn't fatigued anymore and could play with her children and do all of the things that she loved to do but couldn't when she was ill. When she left the office, I told my father-in-law, "I don't need a commission check this month." When I'm able to help people like that, compensation is the last thing on my mind.

I work my business about 20 to 30 hours a week and prefer to keep my home life and my work separate. However, we are building our dream house, which will include an office, which I'm looking forward to working in. I'm usually in the office about 7 a.m. and start my day by studying either the industry or nutrition, for about an hour. Then around 8 a.m. I get on the phone to support and train my downline and work with new prospects. We do this business a little bit differently than most people because we advertise a lot to sell our products. I also set aside a chunk of my day to make follow-up calls.

I call my downline regularly and offer to help them in any way that I can. I have a special note card system so I can readily write down the key points of our conversations and refer to them when I call them back in the future. I talk to a lot of distributors and this system makes it easier for me to service them better. I also have a conference call system in place so I can set up teleconferences with my downline and some of the guys from the corporate team. This answers everyone's questions, keeps us informed and on the cutting edge.

We also have two meetings a month, as well as two major events a year in our area. Being from the mid-western U.S., we've got that whole cowboy mystique thing going which attracts people from around the country. I always joke that it's because everyone wants to see if we all carry guns or something. But they're big events featuring prominent speakers, and they are a lot of fun for the distributors.

The best approach I use when talking to my prospects is eyeball-to-eyeball, and I ask two qualifying questions: The first one is, "Are you interested in making a couple hundred extra dollars each month?" If they say yes, I ask them "Do you have five to ten hours a week to earn that money?" If they say yes to that, I know I've got a qualified prospect. If they say no, I don't pursue them.

Another powerful way I bring in new business builders is to find out what people want and show them how to get it. I use an extremely simple, yet effective, technique to determine their true desire. Once I know what's important to them, I show how my business can help them accomplish those things. It makes for an awesome, nonthreatening approach that benefits everyone.

And, of course, people reject me. But do I get upset? No! Imagine a cruise ship sailing on the ocean. It's beautiful and everyone is happy and out sunning themselves on the deck. Then all of a sudden the sky turns black, the ocean turns gray, the wind comes up, and there's a huge storm. You look over and see these big waves coming up over the deck and sweeping people off and into the ocean. People all around you are drowning you rush, so out onto the deck and throw out one of those rings to save somebody and he looks up at you and says, "I don't like that red and white one, do you have a blue one?" Am I going to stand there and argue with them about why they need to grab the ring? No. I'm going to keep throwing that ring out until somebody grabs it.

It took me a while to figure it out, but network marketing is not a business of convincing people, it's a process of sorting them. If the person answers no to those two qualifying questions mentioned earlier, I won't waste my time with them. Everybody's a suspect, but not everybody's a prospect!

Funny things can happen when you prospect. Once I was talking to a lady, whose last name was Strait, who responded to my ad. When she spelled it out for me I said, "Oh, just like George, the country singer." And she said, "Yeah, he's my son." I replied, "Yeah, right." Then she said, "No really, he's my son!" And sure enough she was from Texas and she really was his mother.

Many new network marketers get scared off when they realize they have to work to make money in this industry. They have an illusion painted for them by unscrupulous folks who tout network marketing as a "get-rich-quick" deal. It doesn't happen like that. When people start a network marketing business they need to dedicate five to seven hours a week to it. Then, by the end of two months they should at least be making what they would be making part-time at Wal-Mart. That's something tangible people can grasp. It's realistic. And when you tell them the truth, you'll have a much higher retention rate.

My advice to those just starting in network marketing is to do things that work. That may seem obvious, but it's amazing how people do so many things that don't work and then repeat them. Realize your mistakes and never ever repeat them.

Also, don't rush into it. You may be excited, but you may not know what you're supposed to be doing. You may be inclined to run out and pitch your friends and family. This often burns your warm market because you're not trained what to say or do. I've seen it many times. Get some training. Confidence breeds competence. Get competent before you go out there with both guns blazing.

Another bit of advice I can give is to make up in volume what you lack in skill. If you're bad at making phone calls, make 50 of them. You might not get anyone to sign up or even listen for that matter, but I guarantee that at the end of those calls you're going to be a lot better at it than when you first started. This gets you out of your comfort zone and forces you to succeed.

Last, be an example for your downline. They do what you do, so make sure they see you doing things that can be easily duplicated. Then they can follow your successful pattern.

Michael J. Krach

"I was willing to pay the price of a career change to get my time back."
Michael J. Krach

Background: Corporate
Year started in networking industry: 1994

Before network marketing, I worked in corporate America as a vice president for a Fortune 150 company. I was familiar with the telecommunications service provider that was servicing the corporation I was with. Based upon their use of a telecommunications product to acquire customers, I became interested in network marketing. That's when I went to an opportunity meeting and "discovered" the industry.

In corporate America I traveled a lot, and I wasn't able to spend the necessary time with my family. I have five children, but I didn't have the freedom to see their basketball games and other school events. So being able to spend quality time with my children was a very motivating, passionate factor for me. I was willing to pay the price of a career change to get my time back.

Now I have control of my time. The financial rewards are better than anything I ever dreamed of. And the thing that was most important to me has now been totally fulfilled.

My family and friends raised their eyebrows a little when they found out I was in network marketing. My brother asked me some questions I couldn't fully answer at first but, nevertheless, he and everyone else were very supportive because of my history of success. So they just said, "Hey, we trust you!" even though it was difficult for me to explain the business and my excitement.

Actually, an asset of mine is that I am very determined. When I believe in something, I can make a passionate commitment. A very high integrity company involved in the deregulation of utilities, tele-

112

communications, and e-commerce formed the basis for my commitment. But there were obstacles. I was used to quicker gratification than what network marketing initially offered me, so I had a bit of a hard time dealing with my slow start. And being in a successful corporate America career, I wanted to do things *my* way. I thought for sure I could come up with a quicker, better way to succeed, but I was proven wrong. I wasn't as coachable as I could have been. I spun my wheels for a while but eventually accepted that there was a system I needed to plug into rather than create my own.

The key ingredient I use to run my business is simply supporting the people on my team, and the best way I do this is leading by example. I personally stay active in all phases of my business since this is a business of duplication.

I make sure that people are enrolled in the company's vision and in network marketing. I focus on helping new reps have quick success. If a new rep "catches on fire" quickly, the momentum is often created for long-term success. Also, prospects are often interested in what your results were during the first 30 to 90 days in the business. It's great to be in the position to share your own success stories and those of others like the ones in this book.

I help them identify and sort potential rep and customer prospects. I conduct three-way calls, conference calls, two-on-one meetings, private business receptions, opportunity meetings, and trainings. I constantly share our high values and philosophy and why consistency and repetition of our daily method of operations is important.

Ongoing telephonic and live exposure to the opportunity, along with training, helps you build belief in yourself and your potential in this business. This also helps you increase your knowledge of the business so you can grow it. I can remember how I initially resisted participation in national meetings, feeling they would probably just be "rah-rah" sessions. After attending the first national meeting though, I understood how the event provided necessary training, networking with other reps, and exposure to top management. These meetings really put you in touch with the "heartbeat" of the company.

Contrary to the typical corporate America approach, I am totally adverse to managing my downline. When I hear that

word I think of controlling them and that's not what I do. Instead, I lead by example and support them. Since so many of us get into the business to get control of our lives, my focus is on leadership versus management. However, I do believe you must "inspect" what you "expect." Therefore, I monitor results to determine appropriate coaching and communication needs.

When prospecting people, I am always looking for someone who has a strong "why"—someone who has a burning desire to change their life in some way. I also strive to determine, to the best of my ability, if they are coachable.

When searching for leaders, I look for something about them which could attract people who would want to be led by them. For example, someone who can inspire others could be a good candidate for leadership. And, I have to feel good about their work ethic. High integrity and persistence are musts!

When I talk to a prospect about my business opportunity, I am very candid. I convey very direct, accurate information about the industry, my company, its products and compensation plan, and our support system. I want a prospect's commitment based upon facts—not hype.

I have such a strong belief in my network marketing opportunity that when someone says they're not interested, I am truly disappointed—*for them*. Most people I identify as prospects can benefit from my network marketing opportunity. However, if I'm rejected I handle it the way it needs to be handled—by leaving it alone. I just say, "next!" But I do go through a checklist to evaluate what I said to see if I could have presented the information in a better way. In total, I haven't had many "down" moments!

Based upon the support of my organization, I put as much time into network marketing as I used to put into my corporate job. But the difference is that my lifestyle and level of enjoyment are much better than they were before. I structure my activities around my personal priorities, especially my family. Helping and watching other people grow in network marketing and seeing them realize their dreams is such a rewarding experience for me. I don't make people successful, but I do believe I help facilitate the process so they can tap into their own capabilities. In short, I help them believe in themselves. I do this because the very belief that a person can achieve and live out their dreams is a powerful thing. I often wonder what would happen if we all realized that about ourselves!

Persistence, consistency, duplication, and hard work are the four major keys to success. I've seen some people quit one step short of success, and it's such a disappointment. Another key is to be coachable. You need to plug in and duplicate the success system. Some people's egos can get in the way and make them feel they need to change the system. But that's what's great about network marketing. There's nothing to figure out because there's a basic, systematic way of doing it.

Sometimes failure in network marketing is a result of unrealistic expectations. Put together a solid, realistic business plan. Map out what activities you need to do over and over on a daily basis and master them. Emulate others who have been successful in the business. Work with your leaders from the very beginning. Once you show them you're willing to work and plug into the system, you will have a lot of people wanting to help you.

And finally, do your best to achieve some success in the first 30 to 60 days. Quick success, no matter how big or small, will keep you motivated! And always celebrate your "victories"!

DREAM ACHIEVERS

Future plans of the Dream Achievers:

73%   To continue in network
        marketing

27%   Retirement, charity
        and/or travel

Euphiazene Linder

"If you want to get rich,
enrich the lives of other people."
Euphiazene Linder

Background: Clerical, Retail, Food Service
Year started in networking industry: 1986

I have an 8th grade education and got married at age 14. I worked for JCPenney counting the money in their vault. Before that I worked as a sales clerk at K-Mart and as a dishwasher at a school cafeteria. My employment at JCPenney was something I was very happy about because I had a sit-down job. Before that, I had worked long hours standing on my feet, which resulted in permanent feet and leg damage. From having my hands in so much water and harsh cleansing agents I also developed a serious skin condition.

During that time, my sister, who is a motivational speaker, had been invited to speak for a company that distributed personal skin care products. After learning about their company and trying the products, she became excited to share this wonderful opportunity with me. When she told me about it I said, "I know where you're leading." I didn't want any part of it.

One Friday, before work, I was recognized as "Employee of the Month." My supervisor took me out to lunch and gave me a 25-cent an hour raise. That Monday, about midday, the JCPenney manager and my supervisor came into the vault and asked if they could speak with me privately. They told me that the company was downsizing and, unfortunately, they were going to have to let me go. I couldn't believe it, especially after they had honored me as "Employee of the Month" and given me a raise!

It was the first time in my life I had ever been dismissed from a job. I was devastated. The worst part was that my husband couldn't work because he was recovering from his second open-heart surgery. This left us both unemployed.

The first thing I did was call my sister for support. Being an eternal optimist, she said, "Euphiazene, you know that when one door shuts another one opens." I didn't want to hear that motivational mumbo-jumbo and wanted to wring her neck! She then told me about a woman named Donna, a single mother with three children, who had become very successful doing network marketing full-time.

My sister put me in touch with Donna and I ordered a starter kit and began using the skin care products. Suddenly, I started getting compliments from people about how much better my skin looked. They wanted to know what I was using. The improvement to my hands was also remarkable. I loved the products and was a walking testimonial!

However, because of my lack of formal education, I was afraid I didn't have the professionalism to be successful. But I became so excited and passionate about telling people how good these products were that I started making four times the amount of money I was making from my job at JCPenney!

I felt great! In fact, I went back to JCPenney to see if they could cash my first *big* check, and they laughed. I didn't go back to brag, but it was a wonderful feeling sharing my success with them. They were all so proud of me and wanted to know more about my business. So I told them all about the products I was selling.

The products are what had me running around like crazy! I couldn't stop selling our skin and body care products. To this day, I have never had anyone complain or return our products for a refund.

I feel fortunate that the people around me were very supportive of my decision to start my own business. My sister was the reason I got into the business, so she was obviously behind me 100 percent. But my husband was concerned about my health challenges, and wondered if I could physically keep up with the demands of building a business.

I love him and understood his concern. But I wanted to build a successful business so that we could have a secure future. I *had* to succeed because my husband was not able to work and I had just lost my job. My motivation was survival, so I felt the fear and did it anyway.

In the beginning I thought I couldn't do network marketing because of my lack of professional skills. I couldn't even type a letter to respond to other leaders in the company. I couldn't see how anyone could succeed in business if they couldn't even type a letter. But I have found that when you don't have secretarial skills, you can make enough money to hire someone who does!

I got over my self-doubt when I started getting those big checks! And my sister, who, in addition to her motivational speaking, has also become president of the company, says, "If money will fix it, it's not a problem; it's only an expense." She also says, "Money's not everything, but it's right up there with oxygen!"

It used to terrify me when I knew I was going to meet with other VPs at our training seminars. I always felt awkward, uncomfortable and out of place. But I found that when I met them, they were wonderful people. Now I feel like I have a whole new extended family.

Once I got enthusiastic about the products and what they were doing for me, I never doubted my ability to sell. I did, however, have a fear of public speaking. Whenever someone would ask for my testimonial story at the meetings, I would be so nervous that my skin would break out in red blotches. But now, because of my love for the business, it doesn't bother me anymore. When I'm up there talking about my success I know I might be inspiring someone else to become successful, too.

I love seeing people achieve their goals. Seeing them walk across the stage, being recognized, and receiving awards is like having your own child succeed. I would much rather have one of my consultants walk across the stage than for me to receive the recognition. I feel tremendous knowing I have played a small part in helping other people succeed and realize their goals.

Because of my physical handicaps, I am often unable to travel to meet with others on my team. But I make up for it by talking on the phone, coaching, training and inspiring everyone I can spend time with. I share sales tips and ways to overcome fear and negativity, and help them raise their expectations of success. I am always there for my people and they know it. I make sure they feel comfortable asking me for advice and help.

When I first got started in network marketing, I put in much more time than I do now. Today I work only about 20 to 25 hours a week.

I motivate my successline by sending out a monthly newsletter and hundreds of encouraging notes and cards to my consultants and management team. As an extra incentive, and to motivate them even more, I have a program where I reward people with gifts and recognition for their sales and sponsoring. I also recognize them in front of their peers when they have done a good job. I've found that people work harder for praises than they do for raises! I have meetings in my home and from time to time in a nearby hotel meeting room. I also attend the major events that my company sponsors across the country and around the world. And I attend as many meetings as possible to inspire my successline.

Thanks to my company's product line, everyone is a potential prospect—they only need to have skin or hair! When I approach them, I follow the three-foot rule. Anyone within three feet is a candidate to hear about my company's products and business opportunity. I give out hundreds of sample packs along with my business card and always ask for their name and phone number. I then follow-up to see if they're interested in being a client or in becoming a consultant and business builder. I always tell them about my success, especially since I've had so many obstacles to overcome.

And, if someone rejects me, I say "next!" There are millions of people who have never heard of my product or company. I hardly think I'll ever run out of prospects!

I love this business because it's fun! Remember, people love to have a good time. During one of my first consultations, the hostess asked if she could have refreshments available for the guests. When I got to her house, the entire table for my product display and demonstration was covered with so much food that it looked like a buffet on a cruise ship. There was no place to set anything like mirrors, product samples or anything else. So I made a joke and said, "As soon as you fill out your orders for the basic products, you can eat." I've never had order forms filled out so quickly and had such delicious food! Everyone left happy.

The keys to success in network marketing are confidence, enthusiasm, persistence, determination and the desire to help other people succeed. This business is about personal development. You're either friendly and caring when you come in the business or you learn to be. The more people you help the more you succeed. You'll have everything you want in life when you help other people get what they want. When you put other people's success before yours, you'll always be able to take care of yourself. If you want to get rich, enrich the lives of other people.

And if you find yourself quitting, you're probably giving up before payday. Most people expect instant success. This is a simple business but, like anything worthwhile, it requires effort. You need to work smart and not let rejection get you down. Most people don't like rejection, and after hearing no five or six times, they refuse to subject themselves to any more of it. They need to understand the law of averages and that eight out of ten people will say no. Remember, you only need a few leaders to build an empire!

Whoever you are, and whatever position you are in, you can do this. I'm not a beauty queen, and I don't wear a size three dress. I don't have a college education, and I'm not a glamorous model who goes around telling people how to sell skin care products. But you know what? None of those things matter.

When you believe in what you're doing and you go out there with enthusiasm, it makes no difference who you are—you can succeed. Give yourself time to grow and build your business, don't prejudge anyone, and don't quit before payday!

Dayle Maloney

*"There are only two ways a prospect is
no longer a prospect: they either join or
you see their obituary in the paper!"*
Dayle Maloney

Background: Newspaper Industry, Sales
Year started in networking industry: 1983

Before I got into network marketing, I was over $250,000
in debt. One day I was listening to the radio and learned
about a seminar to be given by several motivational speakers. I was so excited! Money was really tight but I still bought two
tickets.

My wife, Jeannine, and I attended the seminar. It was a total
sell-out of 15,000 people. At fifteen dollars a ticket, that was
$225,000. I leaned over to Jeannine and said, "I know how to get
out of debt in one day. We'll do the same thing across the river in
St. Paul!" My sales seminar was called the "Dare to Succeed
Rally." I had 17,111 seats and a big line-up of speakers including
Art Linkletter, Bob Richards, Janet Guthrie, Joe Girard, and a few
others. They're the world's greatest salesmen. I was so happy to
have finally figured out a way to get out of debt. My heart could
hardly take the excitement of having $225,000 cash in my hands!

But the day the event finally arrived, we took a tally and realized
we had only sold 7,500 tickets. What I thought would be my financial victory was a financial disaster. That day, I lost another
$91,000 and was now around $350,000 in debt! The morning after
the event I realized that the only people who made money were the
speakers. I told Jeannine, "As of today, I'm a public speaker."

I refused to go bankrupt, so I traveled the country doing small
seminars called, "The Secrets of Selling." While Jeannine and I were
on the road, our home was burglarized. They cleaned us out and took
everything! We started over in a third-floor apartment in St. Paul,
Minnesota. We needed money, so we went back on the road to do

more seminars. When we returned we discovered that we were robbed again! I'd like to say that things got better, but they didn't.

Shortly after that, we were evicted. At age 47, I couldn't pay the $425 rent. I asked Jeannine to call her mother to see if we could move in that night. Two weeks later the engine in my car blew up, so I had to borrow my mother-in-law's car. I had to go from seminar to seminar and sleep in the car.

By this time I couldn't figure out how to get out of debt. I certainly couldn't get a job. I would have to work three jobs for 136 years to earn the amount of money I needed, and I didn't think I'd live that long! We were barely staying afloat and surviving day by day.

In February of 1983, after one of my seminars in Portland, I noticed a woman handing my attendees tapes. She asked if she could hand out free tapes at my upcoming seminars, and since I knew how hard it was to get a business going, I said yes. I was setting up for the second of two seminars in Portland when a man approached me and asked, "Is the woman who was handing out free tapes here?" I told him she would be back later that evening and remembered that I was intrigued about those tapes.

The "tape lady" came back that night and I got one from her. I didn't have a tape player in my car so I sent it to my friend Pat to listen to. When Pat told me about the network marketing opportunity described on the tape, we were excited to join and called the tape lady to learn how to get started. She sent me applications and more tapes and we eventually signed up. That's when my eyes were opened to the network marketing industry. I knew nothing about network marketing, but this woman told me the key was to sponsor as many people as fast as possible. So, that's what I did.

Before network marketing I was a recreation vehicle sales person and a newspaper reporter. I thought I was moving up in the world with my new opportunity, but no one else saw it that way. Once I signed up, I couldn't wait to get home to tell Jeannine how we were going to get out of debt. When I told her it was network marketing, she said, "I married you for better or worse, but not for one of those things." While I set out to make my prospect list, my wife made up a list of people I was *not* allowed to talk to. She called it her "UN-Prospect List" and it said, "No friends, no relatives, nobody you've ever worked with, nobody you went to school with, and nobody within 100 miles of where we live." Everyone laughed at me. So, I made another list called my "In-Spite-Of List." It contained 28 people, and those are the folks I built my business with.

The road of success is always under construction. There were many times when life was tough, but I kept reminding myself that the day I signed the distributor application, I said I would live by six words: *Don't ever learn how to quit.* The first meetings I held were horrible. I once had a meeting at my mother-in-law's house where I invited 30 people. Two showed up. After three minutes one of them said, "Where is the restroom?" He left and never came back.

Another time only two women showed up. After about ten minutes one lady said she felt sick and needed the other woman to take her home. They both left, and I stood there in an empty room. That was the closest I ever got to quitting. But no matter how tough it got, I never quit. I realized that since I was so broke, I *had* to make it happen.

Initially, my involvement wasn't about the products. I needed to get out of debt, so I was looking for an opportunity with a company that had honest management. But the first network marketing company I joined went out of business. All my work was gone overnight. After that, my only criteria for the next company was for it to stay in business! Fortunately I found a company with fantastic products, too.

My greatest obstacle was frustration. I couldn't stand to see people not be successful. I used to sit and cry over it because I thought it was my fault. It took me a long time to realize it *wasn't* my fault. Some people aren't headed for success because they don't do what it takes to succeed. But I tell people how to make failure impossible. If you hold up your end of the deal and put forth the effort, I guarantee you will succeed.

Seeing my own personal growth is the most fulfilling part of network marketing. Getting wealthy in the mind before getting wealthy in the wallet is important. I also love the friendships I've made and watching people fulfill their dreams. I would do it all over again for one-tenth of the money, even if it took five times longer and was ten times the effort.

When I first got started, I was up at 6 a.m. and never went to bed before midnight. I gave this business all it took. I did meetings five or six times a week and talked to everyone about it. I love this business! It gives me a psychological charge that is better than anything I have ever experienced. I have total time freedom and still choose to work my business as much as I do. I have received thousands of letters from people thanking me for helping them change their lives. I can't read them all because I start to cry. My heart feels like it's going to burst from all the emotion.

I constantly encourage my downline with words of advice and motivation. I remind them that since I did it, they can do it too. I do all I can to keep them going.

When I'm looking for business partners, I seek out people who are "above" my level, but I never turn anyone away. My one main requirement is that the prospect has to be breathing. After all, it's not who *you* know, it's who *they* know. I always say that a small hinge can open a big door. In fact, some of the most successful leaders in my organization were sponsored by someone other than myself.

My most effective approach when talking with people about my business opportunity is eyeball-to-eyeball. I say something like, "I have an interesting opportunity I'd like to share with you," and I give it to them directly and honestly. Success is the intention you have when you approach people. Are you simply looking to sponsor someone only to dump them on their own? Or are you looking to build a relationship where you both will benefit?

Rejection used to bother me because I thought it meant I did something wrong. I would blame myself for somebody else's failure. Now rejection doesn't bother me, and yet, I don't burn my bridges. I put the rejecting prospect's name on a list and keep checking back. There are only two ways a prospect is no longer a prospect: they either join or you see their obituary in the paper!

To make network marketing work for you, the key is to just treat people right. Be there for your downline in whatever way they may need you. I say to my prospects, "I refuse to let you fail. If you do your part, I will do my part in return." Realize that although no one works for you, you still need to support them.

Most importantly, don't have false expectations. This happens when sponsors paint too pretty a picture and people join with a misunderstanding of what it takes to succeed. You need patience and discipline because building this business, like any other, takes time.

My advice for those people just getting started in network marketing is to get a dream. It will fuel you to work hard on a day-to-day basis. Then realize it's likely to be challenging, like anything worthwhile is, and you're going to need to give it all you've got. It won't happen overnight—the first check I received in 1983 was for $5.66! But as long as you dream and persist, it can happen for you too.

The rewards for my persistence have been tremendous. My wife and I donated more than $400,000 toward the construction of a new Friendship Baptist Church. My latest project revolves around Dawson McAllister's HopeLine, a telephone crisis center for hurting teens. My goal is to help make this critically important lifeline available to desperate teenagers 24 hours a day, seven days a week, 365 days a year. I am donating the proceeds from my book to this worthy cause.

People may ridicule you and say you're stupid for getting involved in network marketing. Believe it or not, some folks *still* tell me, as successful as I've become, that I'm stupid to be in this business. But those people don't know what they're talking about.

Network marketing is an opportunity to live out your dreams and touch people's lives. There is nothing else like it.

Jimmy Meyer

"If you control your thoughts and you walk, talk, and think the way you would like to become, you will eventually become it."
Jimmy Meyer

Background: Newspaper Industry
Year started in networking industry: 1984

When I was working at the *Daily News*, a guy asked me if I would like to make an extra $500 to $1,000 a month. I was open-minded from the start so he took me to a meeting. When I saw the presentation, I was very intrigued that I could get paid for making other people successful. I studied the guy who was giving the presentation and realized he was successful. I thought that whatever advice he would give me I would take, because if I make money, he makes money. What a concept! It really astounded me.

In spite of my enthusiasm, my family was not supportive of me. When I came home from the meeting I tried to explain what I learned and got it all wrong. My mom thought I was crazy, but some of my friends joined with me. Best of all, when my friends made money, I made more money. The company did such a great job of giving me incentives to work. It didn't matter that I was only 23 years old. I was motivated to earn at least $500 a month.

I'm a big believer that you are one thought away from having a great or bad day. If you control your thoughts and you walk, talk, and think the way you would like to become, you will eventually become it. I'm happy to say that I did move out of my mother's house, got an apartment and eventually bought my first home.

Since I started my business at the age of 23, I had to overcome the obstacle of being young. Because I am in the financial world, I had to prove my knowledge. It was a confidence thing. Once I realized I was doing others a favor instead of the other way around, my business really got off the ground.

The actual daily running of my business begins with this theme: "I must do the most productive thing possible at every given moment." I start out with the six most important things I need to do that day, and then I meet with people for one-on-one presentations. I am constantly prospecting. I don't go out to prospect; I prospect when I am out. My day is judged by how many people I sat down kneecap-to-kneecap with.

I do group presentations about four or five times a week. I also spend a lot of time on the phone. My wife says I have a phone stuck to my ear. I always have a list of the calls I'm making. On the phone I am following up and encouraging people. I believe there are two types of courage: en*courage*ment and dis*courage*ment. All I do is encourage. I check on their activity and attitude. I also do conference calls with different teams I have in the business, and I use our voicemail system which really helps.

I work 24 hours a day seven days a week, but it feels like I'm doing my hobby! I love what I do. My wife and I do this business together. It is incredible. We are playing and working together. I like to call that "Plurking." It puts a smile on my face!

Everyone is a potential teammate for me. Prospects are everywhere! There is no one magic place where all the stars come from. There will never be a test for who can be successful. You've got to cut them open and see what is inside to see if they've got the goodies!

The best way to approach a prospect is to get to know them. I'm on a mission to make friends. I don't want to make a million dollars; I want to make a million friends. I endeavor to find out their hot spots and their purposes. I am a big believer that people quit on their bosses, but they don't quit on their friends.

Seeing other people succeed is such a motivating, fulfilling factor for me. It gives meaning to my mission. When I was new in the industry I heard other people say that, and now here I am saying it. There is nothing better than seeing people fight their obstacles and doubts and succeed.

In fact, this business is all about doing whatever it takes to succeed. One time I was doing a big presentation in a hotel when the fire alarm went off. I was in the middle of the close and had to think quickly. I filed everyone out to the parking lot, got up onto a light pole stand with the light shining on us, and shouted, "Give me one second!" I finished the presentation and even closed people!

People quit network marketing because they stop dreaming. They listen to people who don't do anything with their lives. Doubt is the biggest dream killer. People unplug from the system and they stop showing up. It's sad because so many people quit right before they're ready to explode.

You've got to be bad before you're good, good before you're great, and great before you're outstanding. But before you're bad you've got to start. And when some people start and are bad at it, they can't deal with it because of their pride. That five-letter word is a killer because we are not used to looking silly. We need to learn to laugh at ourselves. I never see failure as failure; rather, it's an opportunity to develop my sense of humor!

There are three main keys to success. First, never give up. Have a sense of urgency, and stay away from negative and cynical people. Have a big dream, do what you don't want to do now so you can do things you want to do for the rest of your life. Get serious about your dream and concentrate on it!

Second, stay plugged in to your upline. Use your upline, but don't abuse them. Using means bringing people to their presentations. Abusing means not showing up to meetings or not bringing anybody. Not being coachable is also abusing them. They have a personal and financial interest in your success. They want you to become successful and they would never ask you to do something that is going to hurt you. That is incredible!

Most of all, be kind to everybody. People always say to me, "You've had so much success and you never change!" They're absolutely right—I don't change! I love working with new people because I can never forget what it's like to be new. If you forget where you came from, it's harder to get where you're going!

Gary and Vicki Morgan

*"We need to tell ourselves
it is okay to be successful."*
Gary and Vicki Morgan

Background: Business Owner, Government, Retail
Year started in networking industry:
Gary 1994, Vicki 1997

Q: What did you do before network marketing?
Gary: I owned a retail store that sold fitness equipment.
Vicki: I worked for the French government in international business development.

Q: How did you get introduced to network marketing?
Gary: I got involved through a friend. I was very skeptical, but I was open enough at the time to look at it. I joined because I saw the market potential of the products and the sincerity of the people involved.

Q: Were your family and friends supportive of your decision to start a network marketing business?
Gary: My family was supportive from the beginning, and some of my friends joined right away because of my enthusiasm. They didn't even understand it all, but that didn't seem to matter.
Vicki: Gary has always been very entrepreneurial. I knew he eventually would do well once he found the right thing for him—something he was excited about. Our friends and family have always seen that in him too.

Q: Did you ever have self-doubt?
Gary: I never doubted that I wouldn't succeed. I saw such a market for the product and I had very high belief.
Vicki: Plus, we put a lot of research into the company. I have had moments where I felt less confident about it, though. My belief in

the product carried me through those moments. I was lucky I found the right company the first time out. Its vision and leadership created an environment I felt comfortable with.

Q: What was your driving motivation to succeed in your new business?

Gary: Time freedom and income potential. I always wanted to wake up in the morning whenever I wanted to, and have the choice to do anything at any time without having to worry about the time or money. Choices equal freedom!

Vicki: Me too. Even though I loved my job and international business, I didn't spend a lot of time with my family. I was sacrificing the most important relationships in my life. Having my time back has allowed me to put more into those relationships.

Q: Did you reach your goals?

Vicki: We have reached some of them. We have an income now for a nice lifestyle. We can live in the house we want to and buy the cars we like. But more important, we can now spend all the time we want with each other. We still have other income goals, but now we have a specific goal for the number of people in our organization to achieve the same or greater level of success that we have.

Q: What were your greatest obstacles?

Gary: I was not very coachable. My way was the right way. I was pretty arrogant! I was very patient with animals and kids but not adults! I also had some self-limiting beliefs that were based more or less on a fear of loss. If you aren't doing well, it isn't that bad because you don't have a lot to lose. But when you start doing well, you're thinking "What is going to go wrong?" We are sometimes self-conditioned. We need to tell ourselves it is okay to be successful.

Vicki: For me it was belief in the industry. It took me three years of being tolerant with all of it before I really looked at network marketing and finally came to believe very strongly in it. Before, when people used to ask me what my husband did, I would make things up because I really didn't understand it myself. I would say he was a marketing director for a "biofoods" company or a nutritional development company. Just anything that made sense from a corporate perspective. I just didn't get it.

Q: What is the most fulfilling part of network marketing for you?
Gary: The most fulfilling part for me is the relationships I have developed. This business is a no-brainer when you really look at it, but it can be frustrating and challenging. I enjoy helping others and seeing people overcome skepticism, take responsibility for themselves and set goals. Once people open their eyes to all the possibilities in front of them, they can never go back to their old ways.
Vicki: Our distributors aren't just business partners; they're family. We care about each other. There is a culture that is developed in network marketing that creates a lot of loyalty.

Q: Describe a typical day/week.
Gary: The daytime is flexible. First and foremost, I enjoy life! I am out prospecting a lot and having coffee or lunch with prospects. I also spend a lot of time on the phone with distributors counseling them, answering their questions and doing three-way calls. Several nights a week we do presentations.
Vicki: I am very involved in prospecting. I spend a lot of time meeting people and I'm always on the phone. I have even joined some charitable organizations so I can meet more people. Most of my time is spent in developing the warm market where Gary spends more time coaching. We still don't put more than 25 to 30 hours a week into this business. We are setting an example for people that they can be successful at this business without overworking themselves.

Q: Do you use meetings and events to grow your business?
Gary: We have home meetings once a week and a large monthly meeting. The rest of the time we do one-on-one presentations and help others do the business. We have a system in place, but we also have flexibility. Some people don't want to go to meetings all the time because they do that all week long in their jobs at other businesses.

You want to have flexibility because if people don't want to do it your way, they can change it to fit their style. People need to start prospecting others with one-on-one meetings, and then follow-up with a group meeting. But if we can't follow-up with them in a group setting, we still follow-up with them! Following up is essential. We want people to be fully informed so they feel comfortable with this business before they join.

Q: Describe how you motivate your downline.
Gary: I don't think you can! It's really up to them, but company events can help because they paint the big picture. I also like to give positive reinforcement of their belief system about the industry—that it is reflective of fine values.

If they are receiving a lot of negativity, I give a supporting word. I let them tap into my enthusiasm about the industry. But ultimately they motivate themselves. I am not there in the morning to make them talk to three people a day. They need to do that by themselves.

Q: How do you deal with rejection?
Gary: You get used to it. Sometimes you want a friend or family member to join so badly, but they say no. Don't take it personally. It could discourage you, but remember, no doesn't necessarily mean no forever!
Vicki: I was used to rejection in my old job from cold calling, but rejection from friends and family is different. No to me means "not right now."

Q: Where do you find your best distributors?
Gary: The best ones are either people we know or referrals. We haven't gone through our entire warm market yet! We still have a long way to go. We are nowhere near what we are capable of.

Q: What is your most effective approach when talking to people about your business?
Gary: I ask a lot of "what if" questions. "What if there was a way you could have...?" "What if there was a way I could show you...?" "What would you do if you had all the money you

needed?" "What will you do when you're done with this job?" "Where would you go if...?" Questions like that help you probe. Ask all those questions and help them dream. I am always shocked at how many people have given up on their dreams.

Q: Is everyone a potential recruit for you?
Vicki: Definitely, but we are not looking to sponsor everyone we meet. We don't want negative people. We are looking to sponsor people who *want* to do this.

Q: How do you do your presentations?
Gary: We have a booklet we use as a guide. But we do our best to convey our enthusiasm and passion in the presentation. We want to connect with the person. We find out what they really want and guide the presentation toward that. We have a "pre-approach" to find out where people are. If their introduction was brief we keep the presentation short. If they have been spoken to in depth, we can spend a lot more time with them.

Q: Why do you think people quit network marketing?
Vicki: A lot has to do with their expectation and belief. They could have both a lack of belief in the industry and in themselves. People need to know up front what is going to happen during their first day, week, and first six months. We tell people ahead of time that their first six months is their apprenticeship, and after one year they can evaluate everything. Also, the barrier to enter the industry is so low that it makes the barrier to quit low as well.
Gary: When I opened my retail store there was no option to quit when things went bad because of the amount of money I put in. I wouldn't even think about quitting because I was fully invested.

Q: What advice could you give to people who are just starting out in network marketing?
Gary: Learn from your mistakes and be open to new information. Enjoy what you do and stay motivated by the big picture!

DREAM ACHIEVERS

FACTOID
#5

Regarding the value of meetings to run a successful network marketing business:

98% believe that holding and attending meetings is essential

2% believe that teleconferencing is just as effective

Merenna and Ted Morrow

*"If you don't have goals, you
won't know where you're going."*
Merenna Morrow

Interview conducted with Merenna only.
Background: Fashion Industry, Pilot
Year started in networking industry: 1966

Before network marketing, Ted was a commercial pilot
and I was a high-fashion model. My mother became a network marketing distributor in 1966, and we realized she was
was doing well and having a good time making money. When Ted
and I were just about to have our first son, he wanted a tax write-off
and I wanted something to do. So my mom signed us up. One day
we received a manual in the mail and, the next thing we knew, we
were in business!

Back then no one understood what network marketing was, so it
wasn't hard for us to approach people with the opportunity. But that
didn't mean it was easy to build an organization. We owe our success to our nutritional products. We have our customers for life
because once they start on the products, they keep using them.

When we started building the business, people didn't understand nutrition. And when we told them they needed to take a food supplement,
they looked at us like we had two heads! They just didn't understand.
So we had to constantly learn about nutrition and then educate people.
Communicating that information was our greatest struggle. But I knew
we would be successful because that's my nature!

Ted and I desperately wanted total independence. And now we
have it. We have always been goal-oriented, so we continually set
new goals. Our ranch is paid for, we have no debts, and our boys
are educated. Those kinds of goals are all done. Our goals now focus on helping other people succeed and develop better lifestyles.

**The most fulfilling part of network marketing is giving peo-
ple the opportunity to succeed.** I love helping people. It's an

avenue you can't take in the corporate world. Also, a high percentage of millionaires come from the network marketing industry. You don't get that in the corporate world either.

One of our distributors lived in a small apartment in Manhattan, drove an old Volkswagen Bug and was $40,000 in debt. That person now lives in a house on an 80-acre lake in Georgia and is building a retreat on 300 acres in North Carolina! I love seeing that. Helping people succeed is very special to me.

My typical day begins by going to work early in the morning and making ten calls to my distributors by 10 a.m. I call it my "10 by 10" rule. Then I talk to new people about my business. I stop working by 3 or 4 o'clock and go exercise. My company holds meetings a few times a week and I always go to them. We also do a lot of traveling and visiting our distributors throughout North America, Canada and Europe. No two days are alike. There is always something different happening.

Since I have so many people in my organization from all over the world, there is no way I could possibly be in touch with each one of them on a constant basis. That's why we have monthly conference calls. One month the call may be product training, while another month's call may be motivational in nature. We also have retreats where we motivate distributors by awarding them pins to recognize them for their accomplishments. Recognizing distributors is very important.

I spend eight to ten hours a day in my office. However, this is a 24-hour a day business, so I might make calls early in the morning or late at night. This is my life!

Ted and I offer our opportunity to everybody. We have no criteria for approaching people. Everyone has their own needs and ways of getting there. But we have found that everyone needs our products. So, by sharing the products we find our business leaders.

My best approach when talking to prospects is to simply ask, "If I could show you an opportunity that could let you stay home with your children, would you listen?" Then I share the products. In fact, I give a lot of products away! Some people say they don't feel well in general, so I give them some supplements to make them feel better. Then I ask them to contact me if they want more, and they do.

Rejection was very hard for me when I first started. I was crushed when someone didn't want to listen. I felt as if I was failing because I wasn't getting my message across. It was hard getting past that. Now I deal with it by having an answer for everything! I have an arsenal of information for people, and since I have a better understanding of the company and nutrition now, it makes my job easier. It's a constant learning process.

The keys to a successful network marketing business are to be professional at all times, have a focus or a dream to keep you on track, and most importantly, to laugh! In fact, we laugh all the time! When we started our business, we were doing health fairs. Once we were in a very posh hotel in Manhattan, and the bellman started helping us carry our products inside, which were in large cardboard boxes. He was in a bad mood to begin with and wasn't happy about doing this for us. He was going up the steps when, all of a sudden, one of the boxes broke. Vitamins went rolling everywhere...down the steps, into the lobby, and all over the place. The bellman was now absolutely livid. But we laughed about it because it looked so funny in such an upper-crust hotel!

The most challenging thing to teach new distributors is that network marketing isn't easy. It's a challenging business, and people can get discouraged because of the rejection they receive. They also may not have a strong upline. It's a shame to see people quit when they don't get immediate success. Ted and I didn't get to where we are in just one or two years. It was a slow, steady process. It's not a flash in the pan type of business. It takes time and determination.

If you're just starting out in network marketing, you need goals and a clear focus. If you don't have goals, you won't know where you're going. Also, make a commitment to make it work by sticking with it and staying positive! A good attitude builds confidence and reading inspirational books, like this one, helps tremendously. Above all else, always remember that *you* control your destiny!

Jeff Nicholls

"Network marketing has not only made me a lot of money, it has also given me rare and meaningful moments that, as an accountant, I probably would never have experienced."
Jeff Nicholls

Background: Accounting
Year started in networking industry: 1986

A friend of mine from a real estate office in Denver came in one day with a cassette tape from a network marketing company that seemed to fit my background. Unfortunately, it was one of those things that looked good on paper but didn't really work. That company lit my fire though, and made me discover that the concept of network marketing could really work.

Some years later, another person I knew sent me information on the company I'm with now. Since I'm a numbers guy, I know a lot about marketing plans. When I saw the company's compensation plan I thought it was solid and workable. I also thought the products were exceptional. The products are the glue that holds a network marketing company together. The consumption of the products will generate your income, so they must be far better than what you can find in any store.

With the compensation plan and products in place, I became a distributor, and that's a decision I'm quite proud I made!

A few people I knew were supportive, but for the most part everyone else thought I was crazy. They questioned my sanity and didn't understand why I would fiddle around with this stuff when I had so many other things to do.

But there were two things that drove me. The first was to completely control my own destiny. I was tired of somebody else deciding what my tomorrows would bring. I worked for some nice people, but when it came right down to it, they didn't really care about what would happen to Jeff Nicholls.

The second thing was to work with people. I love teaching, training and working with others and giving them new ideas.

I did have some self-doubt, though. I realized this was a challenging business. To get over that doubt, I read every book about network marketing I could get my hands on and I retrained and remotivated myself whenever I had the chance. This book, for example, is something I would have read over and over again to keep inspired. It gives you confidence when you read about how others overcame obstacles and became successful in this business.

Nowadays my inspiration comes from my downline. I recently had a gentleman tell me that because of the opportunity I offered him, his wife was able to quit her job and stay home with their children. He said that they could never have done that if it weren't for me. You can imagine how I felt when he told me that! It's just so neat to see somebody make such a positive change in their life and to know I had something to do with it.

This truly is an amazing business. Network marketing has not only made me a lot of money, it has also given me rare and meaningful moments that, as an accountant, I probably would have never experienced. I've been on a Safari in Africa. I'm going to Austria, Italy, Germany and Switzerland next year, and I've also been to the Caribbean a few times.

When you first hear about a network marketing opportunity and talk to your sponsor, they very rarely mention the traveling that's possible. The money is great, but it's incredible to be in a car six feet away from a lion in Africa. I even have photographs of an elephant tearing down a tree just to get to a small piece of food on a twig! I never would have been able to go on that trip without my network marketing business.

My day starts by getting out of the house by 7 a.m. I have a small office outside the home. Although I recommend others to work at home, I need that separation between my personal and business lives. In my office I spend a huge amount of time on the phone doing conference calls and three-way calls. I also meet with people every day for one-on-one presentations, but the bulk of my day is spent on the phone. And sometimes I work as late as 10 p.m.

I spend a lot of time motivating my downline. Also, our company has a voicemail system, so I leave messages for them a few times a week. I introduce my downline to industry publications. I also run my own contests for them that reward people for achieving small goals. I do lots of little things, but I know that strong relationships are what make this business work. I'm always in contact with my organization to support them and keep their motivation high.

I have also found that laughter is a great motivator. You will have a lot of good times in network marketing because people are working for themselves. There are no bosses, so people are more relaxed with each other.

Meetings also play a big part in my organization's operation. I make sure to attend all of them! The meetings are a place for distributors to bring their guests and learn more about the opportunity and business basics. The company also has regional meetings that take place three or four times a year. Conference calls happen frequently as well.

I don't prejudge when I prospect and I talk to almost everybody. There are some things, however, that I do avoid. For instance, if someone can't pay their rent this month, I don't approach them. Although you can make money fairly quickly, this is a business that takes some time and money to get going. So I tend to approach people who have a job but want a change.

When I approach my prospects, I talk about lifestyle. When people ask me what I do for a living, I tell them I help people retire early so that they can spend time with their families. The money is great, but it's just a bridge to a lifestyle of time freedom. When I say that, I almost always get their attention and they ask to hear more. That's when I say, "Let me ask you a question. If I could show you a way to make six, seven, eight thousand dollars or more a month, working seven to ten hours a week, would you give me 30 minutes to hear about it?" If they say yes, I set an appointment with them.

Early on in my network marketing experience, I took rejection personally. It was tough, but today I realize there are many different kinds of people in the world and I see it as a timing situation. Everyone needs an opportunity like this. So, if someone says no, I just stay in touch and keep checking back. I contact them every six months until they either say yes or die!

The one thing that will surely make you succeed in network marketing is a burning desire to make a change and make a difference in your life. You also need a commitment to face long-term goals and possess a willingness to learn.

If you feel as though you're not getting anywhere in your business, it could be because you're letting the dreamstealers get to you. This happens to a lot of people. Unfortunately, people let their friends and family—people who often don't know anything about network marketing—convince them that they can't succeed. Since they may not be all that strong in the first place, that may ultimately bring them down.

But think about it: if a family member needed brain surgery, would you go talk to a plumber to find out the best way to go about it? Of course not, but that's what some people do when they first look at network marketing. When new distributors have questions, they, for some reason, go to their family and friends to get the answers. But they need to talk to successful network marketers instead. If they have realistic expectations and stay focused, they can get past the dreamstealers.

It is imperative to write a solid set of goals down on paper and share them with someone whom you respect. When you do that, in your mind you will be accountable to those goals. You won't be able to rationalize or back out of them as easily as you could if you had kept your goals a secret.

The next thing you need to do is get together with your upline to put together a daily set of actions to follow. If you're going to only work three days a week, you need to plan what you will do on those three days. You need a business plan for any business you run. If you don't make one, your time will be spent inefficiently. Learn as much as you can about your company and the industry, and then commit to working at it for at least a year.

Dennis Nun

*"I have accepted the philosophy that you
don't help people who need the help;
you help people who want the help."*
Dennis Nun

Background: Student
Year started in networking industry: 1973

My father was a farmer in Nebraska when a friend of his approached him with a network marketing opportunity. My dad then referred his friend to me. At the time I was in college full-time and working two jobs. My wife, Patty, was also working. We had the same problem most people do—"too much month left at the end of the money." So, I was interested enough to take a look at what my dad's friend had to offer.

I was invited to a business opportunity meeting where I learned all about what network marketing could do for me. I left feeling a bit excited, and the next time the meeting was held I brought Patty so we could look at the business together. She thought it was fine as long as she didn't have to "keep the books." So we began as part-timers in addition to everything else we were doing. Eventually my father also became a distributor and we began using and selling the products together.

Patty was not very enthusiastic at first, but she was very supportive. The rest of the family mostly became customers. In general, they weren't negative, but they certainly weren't as thrilled as I was about the opportunity to build a successful network marketing business.

By the time I finished graduate school a year and a half later, my income from my network marketing business was comparable to any of the job offers I had. So naturally I went full-time! That was in December of 1975. Our income doubled every year the first six years after that, and it has continued to increase every year since.

Network marketing was such a different concept and I did have to adjust to certain challenges. I remember hearing somewhere that people typically run into two or three good opportunities in their lifetime. I thought if that's the case, then I have to get over the hurdles and keep taking the risks. I really had nothing to lose. Today I can't figure out why so many people just don't understand it. Everyone needs to do this business!

My driving motivation to succeed was survival. Initially, we were just hoping it would be enough to take care of the food and some bills. But a friend in our upline asked me if I would be willing to work this business for four or five years, without seeing much success, if it paid substantially in the future. I thought about it and realized that most people are just getting by as it is, and so were we. So I said yes and made the commitment to work as hard as I could for five years. During those years we were happy to see the business grow as steadily and successfully as it did, and today the opportunity is better than it was when we first got started!

But it wasn't easy. There were times when I was my own worst enemy. Sometimes I was too hard on myself and needed to relax. If there's one thing I learned, it's that you need to enjoy the process of network marketing and delight in the progress. This is a great way of life when you realize there will be ups and downs.

I typically work only three days a week. One of those days is spent organizing and planning. The other two days I spend calling prospects, talking to my key distributors and conducting opportunity meetings. I also do home meetings and one-on-one presentations. In all, it comes out to about 25 to 40 hours of work.

The way you support your downline is to tell them to call you. Every great leader will give you that same advice. Your distributors don't work for you, so you can't really manage them. But you can encourage them and be there for them when they need you. Personally, I am guilty of overkill. People tell me that all the time. So I had to eventually learn to not manage my distributors.

Recognition is also a great way to motivate a downline. Letting people know you appreciate their efforts is worth so much. I recognize my distributors in various ways. I run occasional contests and offer prizes, use voicemail messages, and mail a newsletter where I list their names often. I motivate them because I care about them.

When it comes to recruiting, I am a product person. I always tell people about our products. I am also constantly passing out cassette tapes to prospects, since I find this approach very effective. I have adopted a system of using these tapes to help me find the people who are looking for a business opportunity.

If a prospect comes back and tells me they're not interested in the business, I simply move on and ask someone else. Rejection is something I expect. It's just part of the process.

I heard once that you can maintain a positive attitude by having a negative assumption. You just assume that nine out of ten people are not going to be interested. They're not bad people, they're just not going to make good business partners. I have adopted the philosophy that you don't help people who need the help; you help people who *want* the help.

I find that a lot of new distributors quit network marketing because they expect too much too soon. They don't recognize the amount of work that's required to build a successful business. If someone quits, it's easy to blame the company for not succeeding. You know, the "I tried that once and *it* didn't work" defense. But what they're really saying is that their expectations weren't met based on their performance.

The bottom line is persistence. If you keep working, it works! It may not seem like it, but there really is no wasted effort. Another key is to be teachable. You need to be a student of the industry and continue to learn. And always strive to improve your techniques. I love the saying, "When you're green you grow, when you're ripe you rot." That's the plain truth.

Be a student. Get educated. There's nothing new to reinvent in this industry. It's all been done before and your job is to do your best to fully learn and duplicate it all. Just never throw in the towel!

Ken and Shirley Pontious

*"People don't care how much you know
until they know how much you care."*
Ken Pontious

Interview conducted with Ken only.
Background: Real Estate (Ken);
Shipping and Transportation (Shirley)
Year started in networking industry:
1976 (Ken); 1991 (Shirley)

A ll my life I wanted to be successful. My father constantly put me down. He told me I wouldn't make anything of myself and that I would be a bum. That simply made me want to be the best I could possibly be. So, in any business I started, I had to be at the top. My father has since realized his mistake, but I wonder if I would be where I am now if that hadn't happened.

Before network marketing, I was a real estate rep and then owned my own real estate brokerage firm. During that time I was introduced to the industry by an orthopedic surgeon. I asked him why, with his income, he was interested in network marketing. He told me that if anything happened to his hands, his income would stop. I then looked at the real estate industry and realized my income also would stop if something happened to me!

The company I'm with now is my ninth in 21 years! When my family and friends saw me work so hard, only to be let down when some of the early companies went out of business, they wondered why I stuck with it. There were times I wondered too. I had relatives and friends who didn't want me to succeed because they were afraid I wouldn't associate with them anymore if I did. They realized that if I reached my goals, my lifestyle would change—you know, travel, cars, and all that stuff. So, without realizing it, they tried to pull me down.

Because of all that, I came close to quitting, but decided I would do it one last time. And I'm thankful I did. In my first year with this company I earned $800,000, and in my second I made $2.3 million. Of course, now all my relatives are very supportive. You know how that goes!

The most fulfilling part of network marketing for me is seeing people stretch their abilities and achieve their dreams. I have met some people who were so shy that they couldn't even speak. Over a period of time you watch their self-esteem grow and they become a leader and run a successful business. You need to love people to do well in network marketing.

The majority of my day is spent doing three-way calling. People use me when they feel they can't talk to someone who earns a high income or is a successful network marketer. My wife Shirley and I also put the VIP Educational System together, which is a complete approach on how to build the business. We have spent a lot of time this past year putting that together.

You can't motivate people. They need to motivate themselves. You know the old saying, "You can lead a horse to water, but you can't make it drink." What you *can* do, though, is give the horse salt so it will want to drink! You need to recognize, excite, and encourage people so they can believe in themselves.

By doing this they feel they can do things they never thought were possible. My downline needs to see the example I set. I never had a lot of help when I started, so I wanted to help the people in my group. I feel they deserve all I can give them. This business is really about people helping people.

I always made it a point to have lunch with the top network marketers around the country. I wanted to meet them, learn from them and share ideas. But, my success didn't come from finding the right people. It came by being the right person. Everyone who became a top leader in my organization actually called and asked *me* to sponsor them. Remember, you attract the right people when you become the right person.

My approach with a new prospect is to lead with the opportunity and validate with the product. And I have had great success with that. Also, I like to ask people questions. People don't care how much you know until they know how much you care. I listen to people and learn about their dreams and goals. I ask them, "If you were totally out of debt right now, what is it that you would like to do with your family?" I find people are so beat down nowadays that they have a hard time answering.

Sometimes I need to ask that question a couple of different ways. Then I do my presentation. At the end I ask them, "With my help and support, can you understand how we are going to be able to help you?"

My presentations are very conversational, and I use a seven-step approach that I learned over 14 years ago. First I talk about "Dreams." I get people thinking beyond their poverty. Second is the "Industry." I tell them up front about network marketing. Third is "Company Management," where I talk about the stability of my company. Fourth is the "Products." Here, I help them see and believe that the products are of value. Fifth is "Compensation." They need to believe they can make money with my opportunity. Sixth is the "Support System." Here I get them to answer the question, "Can I do this business?" And seventh is the "Close." The best way to close a prospect is to refer back to his or her dreams and goals.

Even more importantly, I am believable. I am not the most eloquent speaker or handsome guy in the world, but people tell me I am believable and that I tell the truth. They say I put them at ease.

The people who quit network marketing are disillusioned. I show them on a graph why people fail. I explain how someone new in the industry, even if they are working it consistently, won't become rich overnight. I show them that when they stay in and build the business, they will eventually make money. People can accept the truth right up front, so just be open and honest with them.

My first check in this company was $67, but now I make more money in a month than the President of the United States makes in a year, *doubled!* So this industry *does* work. It's exciting for me to get up each morning and work with my wife Shirley, the love of my life and my partner too. Together we built a business that will continue providing for me and my family. If you give up before you're making a lot of money, then you haven't given yourself a fair shot.

People nowadays are stressed out, beaten down, and worried about job security. Those who have financial success in their jobs often don't have a lot of *time* for their families. Yes! It's a great time to get into network marketing. If you want more out of life, get involved and stick with it!

Network marketing is a tremendous opportunity and has enabled me to do things in life I never thought I *could* do. My wife and I recently gave money to a girl's school for a new roof. We also gave $100,000 to a private high school. We noticed how committed the teachers were, yet some of them were only getting room and board and $400 a month. We felt they deserved more than that. We just received a letter stating that they named the educational wing of the school after us.

Shirley and I are where we are because of a lot of great people, so we want to keep giving back. And we are able to do so because of the great organization we have been able to help grow into what it is today. What a pleasure having peace of mind from a business that my wife and I can work and build together, while receiving a phenomenal long-term income.

This industry has been so good to me that I can never see myself retiring. In fact I'm having so much fun, I feel like I'm retired already! So, grab hold of this opportunity and make it happen—*for you!*

*　　*　　*

On Sunday, September 26, 1999, Ken passed away due to complications from the side effects of medication taken in his battle against a brain tumor. This left an emotional void in the people involved in the business. "To the end, Ken's thoughts and concerns were about those he loved and not himself," said his wife, Shirley, in a statement sent to the thousands of distributors in their organization. Shirley worked hand-in-hand with Ken in building their business. She will continue her commitment to and leadership of their group, including the VIP Educational System and TEAM Paragon.

Even where there is adversity, there is hope; where there is sadness, there is optimism; and where there is uncertainty, there is adventure! Notwithstanding Ken's passing, because of the sincerity and integrity we both held so dear, TEAM Paragon has gone from strength to strength. We have opened in five new markets, making 14 countries all together! We have also opened an 8,000 sq. ft. facility as home office for the VIP Educational System. And leaders from almost all the top companies have come to join us, and business is booming.

Ken's affect on the company, its employees and distributors, and the network marketing industry as a whole, was immense. His legacy is not just living on…it's flat out charging forward!

Pamela Nicole Randisi

"You'll eventually make it if you believe in what you're doing and never give up!"
Pamela Nicole Randisi

Background: Secretarial
Year started in networking industry: 1976

When I was an executive secretary at General Motors, I went to a neighborhood skin care class as a favor to a friend. I was very skeptical and I really didn't want to go, but I went and tried the products and loved them. Within two weeks I became a consultant. I thought if I loved the products so much, other people would too.

I didn't think I was going to be exposed to such a wonderful company and high-quality product line, especially our signature anti-aging product. After one use I believed in this product and I still feel that way today. You need to be proud of what you're representing to build a successful network marketing business.

My family has always been in business for themselves, and they saw this as an opportunity for me to be in business for myself. My mother used to sell skin care and cosmetics while I was growing up, and she was very successful. So she understood my decision to become a beauty consultant.

My father had always encouraged me to start a business and my friends were supportive as well because they loved the products.

No matter how much support you have, you will always have ups and downs just like any other business. If someone cancels an order or postpones a class, you may begin to have small doubts. I would listen to motivational tapes and read positive thinking books to keep my spirits up. When things would not go as well as expected, I was determined to *never give up.*

Having to relocate out of state three times and rebuild my business each time was hard, especially being a single parent, but I just kept at it and *never gave up*. The important thing for me was to stay focused and move forward.

In the beginning, money was an issue, but that wasn't why I pursued this. In fact, I doubt that you could truly be successful in network marketing if money is your only concern. When I joined I wanted no pressure but loved incentives. I enjoy helping people look good and feel good about themselves, as well as seeing them become financially independent. It's important for me to make a positive difference in people's lives.

There isn't a better feeling than seeing someone else grow. The more I help people grow the more I am motivated to keep on doing this. Since our products and program are so great, I know I'm offering people something good for them and making a positive difference in their lives.

My life has definitely changed over the years. When you begin your business, you spend the first few years building your base of consultants. You eat, sleep, and breathe network marketing. I was a skin care consultant 24 hours a day! I seized every opportunity. I was talking about skin care and makeup constantly!

Today it's very much the same. The key is doing the same things over and over and sticking with it. It's a very positive, empowering lifestyle.

For instance, we have meetings to recruit and to train. They are very important to people and become part of their lifestyle. They learn the business while having fun.

In the beginning, I worked very hard and still do. But now it's a way of life. People have asked me how much time I spend doing this. All I can say is that I work a lot because I like it so much and I really believe in what I'm doing—helping people. It's a win-win situation.

An important key in my success is that my consultants know I am no different than they are. I lead by example and fully believe in what I'm doing. I also keep in constant communication through phone calls, postcards, and meetings. I'm always involved with them in one way or another. I work with people who show a strong interest and have a burning desire to really make it work.

I tell all my consultants to approach absolutely everybody with the product line! How many people do you know who have skin? Everyone! Well, that's who can use our products! For me, approaching people is easy. I'll say, "Have you heard of my company?" If they say "no," I'll say, "You haven't? Oh, we've just got to get together!" Then I quickly get their name and number and I give them mine. That approach has always worked very well for me.

Since I was raised with a positive attitude, I don't take rejection personally. There are billions of people on this planet and there's plenty of business around for everyone. I've learned that people are not rejecting me when they say no. And my conviction in my product and company is stronger than ever now, so it's difficult for people to say no to me today!

To be successful in network marketing, people need to develop a positive attitude, knowledge of their product (knowledge is empowering; ignorance is expensive), and a burning desire to succeed. You will make it in network marketing when you believe in what you are doing and never give up. Most people have never done network marketing. When they get into it, they might feel awkward at first; and since it may not feel quite so comfortable right away, they may want to quit.

You, too, may feel awkward at first and it may take some time for you to get used to it. But realize that you have made a decision that can change your life in ways you've only dreamed of. Network marketing is a very simple business. The challenging part may be staying motivated and just doing it.

Someone has given you an opportunity for an extraordinary lifestyle through network marketing; now use all the product(s) and services in your line so you can believe in them, go out and tell others, and never give up. Then you, too, can become a Dream Achiever!

DREAM ACHIEVERS

When asked if their family and friends were supportive of their decisions to start network marketing businesses:

53% Yes

47% No

Anita Rawls

"Enthusiasm is contagious!"
Anita Rawls

Background: Banking
Year started in networking industry: 1991

During my banking career, I wanted financial freedom and to spend more time with my family. I started researching the market and discovered network marketing. I realized very quickly that the banking industry was not going to get me the financial freedom I thought I deserved. Many times in the banking environment, males and females are not compensated equally, and I always felt a little bit underpaid. However, I knew that with network marketing I could make as much money as I wanted without there being a glass ceiling.

After a couple of attempts with unsuccessful companies, my friend Bill called me and introduced me to the company I'm now with. I discussed the opportunity with my husband, Prince, and he said, "If Bill's doing this, follow him." Neither he nor I have regretted that decision!

A solid network marketing business is built on consumable products so there can be repeat monthly volume. Nobody will continually buy a faulty product. I felt that my company's product line was unsurpassed, so it was easy for me to stand behind it.

My husband has always been 1,000 percent behind me from the get-go. And while my extended family, and my mom and dad and brothers initially looked down on me a bit, they don't anymore!

I have no problem admitting that when I first started I questioned my ability to succeed. I was not successful with my first two network marketing opportunities. One of them went under and the other one had a terrible compensation plan. Those factors weren't my doing, but they did cause some doubt. So I had to give myself an attitude adjustment.

In the beginning, rejection was a problem for me. I had to learn that if my prospects said no, the opportunity simply wasn't right for them at that time. It wasn't because of me. I teach my people that no is never a no until the prospect dies!

My love in life is to be able to help people. And being in the antiaging business I know that I can improve their health and wealth at the same time. As long as I can keep that in mind, rejection really doesn't get to me.

When I meet someone for the first time, I always ask, "What business are you in?" If I ask the question first, then I know they are going to respond back to me with the same question. When they do, I say, "I'm in the health and wealth business. Which are you interested in?" Or I'll say, "I work with an antiaging company," and that immediately prompts a question from them. So both of these answers get me talking about the business.

I used a new interest-generating statement the other day. I ran out to my mailbox when the mailman just happened to be walking toward it. He handed me the mail, and I said, "Oh! Thanks for bringing me my paycheck!" He responded by telling me that he got paid yesterday, and he actually told me the amount of his check. So I said, "Well, add x-thousand to that and you'll have my paycheck!" He immediately started asking questions. I gave him a starter pack of our weight-loss products, and a few hours later he was back ringing my doorbell wanting more information. So the products are a fabulous way to share the opportunity as well!

Typically I work about 70 hours a week. My day starts around 6:30 a.m. I take three hours for myself, doing household chores, tending to my yard, running errands, and taking personal motivation time. Then, by 9:30 or 10 a.m., I go into my office, which is in my home, and spend the next half of my day on the phone with my organization answering questions, and motivating and encouraging them. The other half of the day I spend doing my own recruiting.

My husband gets home at 7:30 p.m. and then we have dinner. But after that I'm right back on the phone until about 10 p.m. I don't have fixed office hours because I turn my phone on and off when I choose.

I constantly share motivational encouragement and support with my downline, encouraging them to believe in themselves. I also give them support by teaching them the importance of a positive mental attitude. However, each of them also needs to be self-motivated and have the desire to make life-changing decisions.

I never manage my downline. Instead, I coach them. You walk a fine line there because each of us is in business for ourselves, and no one works for anyone. I want each and every one of them to be more successful than what they think they have the capability of doing. So when I put a person into the organization, my attitude is that they are going to the top and I work accordingly. I never act like a manager. Instead, I encourage them to forge ahead.

Having meetings my distributors can attend is absolutely essential. We have them on a weekly basis and I attend all of them. You can't build a business without them! Meetings are a place to keep learning and keep the motivation going. That means a lot coming from me, because in the beginning I didn't like them. I hated feeling that I had to be somewhere each week. But now I know that they are essential to my success!

The greatest success tool available is your love for what you're doing. A genuine love for your company and product(s) will fuel you like a rocket. You'll find yourself working harder than you ever have in your life, and that can only result in success. You also need persistence and enthusiasm. I have a saying that says, "Enthusiasm sells; logic smells." Enthusiasm is contagious! Last, you need to set goals. Put them in writing and read them daily.

Most people quit network marketing because they don't *see* the opportunity, they don't *believe* they can do it, and they don't step out of their comfort zone enough to do what it takes to succeed. They don't see the big picture. Many people have heard the expression, "You can be given a fish to have dinner tonight, or you can be taught how to fish to have dinner every night." New distributors sometimes don't understand the duplication process and they quit. It's the easy way out.

I always go back to the book, *Think and Grow Rich,* where Darby was mining for gold with no success. He quit and sold his equipment to a junkman. The junkman hired an expert who informed him to keep mining; he mined three more feet and struck one of the richest gold mines ever. This story always sticks in my mind. I know I am just three feet away from finding that next person who will make my business explode!

Whatever happens in your business, don't quit. Quitting will get you nowhere in life. Time is moving forward whether you want it to or not, so make the decision to do something magical with it now before it races right by you.

Ray Robbins

"There's no better feeling than being a part of someone else's happiness."
Ray Robbins

Background: Military, Pilot, Real Estate, Retail
Year started in networking industry: 1982

Before network marketing I had many different jobs, but none of them made my life as full and exciting as network marketing has. I have been in the amusement vending business, the real estate business, the retail management profession, and in the military as a major and a helicopter pilot.

Some of my church friends approached me and told me about something they were doing on the side to make a little extra money. They thought the product line was very good but, like a lot of people, I was very nonreceptive for quite some time. I finally went to an opportunity meeting and found out that I liked the concept of network marketing.

But the thing that really clinched it for me was the product line. I am product driven. Somebody had to prove to me that the products were viable and that you couldn't get them anywhere else. The fact that I'm involved with my company means I really believe in our products!

I thought everyone would be happy about the decision I made, but I was surprised to find out the opposite was true. There's a very strong negative tone that exists throughout America regarding network marketing, and a lot of the people I knew felt the same way.

But the longer I was involved, the more supportive they all became. And the more successful I became the more they realized network marketing does work. Today I have a lot more support than I did in the beginning, and some of my friends and family are now in my business. I had a cousin who once thought that anyone who did network marketing was a second-class citizen but, after witnessing my success, he has decided to do it too.

I have always loved to be involved with things where I see many people benefiting. I've been the president of a school board, and have built a new YMCA in my city. I've even been the chairman of an organization for abused kids. It excites me to see people improve their lives. That's why I'm in network marketing. I get to help people improve their health and create better lives. It's what I look forward to every day of my life.

To be successful you need to stay motivated. One look in your bookstore's self-help section will lead you to books that can help you raise your self-confidence. If you read a number of them about the network marketing industry, as well as other books that are inspirational and informational, you'll find yourself in a positive, rather than doubtful, state of mind.

The biggest obstacle for me was that the people I knew were strapped financially. So, they didn't even have enough money to get started, let alone buy sales aids or the products on a regular basis. Therefore, I did all I could to educate them about our products. I created a value and a need to get them interested in buying. Once they finally tried the products and realized how fantastic they were, I explained how they could get the products free simply by introducing the business opportunity to others. It didn't work all the time, but it did work.

Each day I start early, end late, and cram in a lot of work in between. My business demands my attention, so I give it my all! I work close to 100 hours a week and that's a lot. But most people don't have to work that hard, or even half that hard, to be successful in network marketing! I most definitely classify myself as a workaholic. And although I consider that my weakness, I'm not complaining! I overdo it, I know, and I'm making an effort to slow down.

I travel considerably to meet with my distributors and I give presentations all the time. I really don't think that description would intrigue most people to get into network marketing. The difference between what I do and the work most people do is that I have a tremendous amount of fun. I absolutely love what I'm doing.

My number one key to success in network marketing is to go to meetings. People who go to meetings every week are more likely to become successful. However, don't rely solely on meetings either. You need to apply what you're learning and do phone calls and one-on-one presentations. But the meetings act as a catalyst for all the other things to fall into place. The meetings repeatedly remind you of why you're in the business and what you need to do to make a success of it, as well as give you an opportunity to associate with others who are moving on.

I motivate my downline and lead them by setting an example. When they see me do something, they're inclined to do it too. Also, I communicate constantly with them and meet with them face-to-face whenever possible. I don't do it because I have to, I do it because I *want* to.

When I approach people about my business opportunity, I look at everyone as a potential recruit. Everyone can use at least one of our products, but I don't necessarily think everyone can do this business. It becomes apparent fairly quickly who is excited about the business and the products, as opposed to those who are just excited about the products.

When I talk to a prospect, the first thing I do is share our products. I just choose one product that will "fit" the person well. For example, we have a children's product, which supplies a child with vegetables via a gummy bear. If you're talking to a mom, that would be an ideal product to key in on. She can then make sure her child is consuming vegetables. And if I'm talking to a 50-year-old, I'll talk about the products that can give them energy and a sense of well-being. It's easy to share the products when you consider your prospect first.

I don't have any concerns about rejection. I accept a no just as readily as a yes. It is a person's prerogative to make a decision, and I'm fully aware that not everyone I approach will say yes.

To make the most of your network marketing business, attend all the meetings and events you possibly can. Also, educate yourself—know your products and opportunity inside and out. Why does a heart surgeon make a million bucks a year? Because he or she studied and learned about the medical craft. I am a strong *dis*-advocate of the "keep it short and simple" theory. Learn, re-learn, and learn some more. That's the only way to develop an arsenal of information to help you share your opportunity with others. Not having that arsenal of information is a major reason why people quit the industry.

Also, set goals that are activity-oriented. A bad goal is, "I want to make a thousand dollars next month." A good goal is, "I'm going to a meeting every week to learn as much as I can," or "I will share my opportunity and products with all of my family and friends."

There is a story I usually end my presentations with. It's about a Harley Davidson motorcycle I owned while in college. I could never understand why sometimes it would fire up when I'd kick-start it six times, yet other times I would have to kick it 30 or 40 times. So I kept a whole bunch of statistics to figure it out: the time of day, the temperature, the amount of gas in the tank, the last time I rode it—anything I could think of recording. I wanted to some-how, scientifically, figure out why it wouldn't start the same way every time.

I finally discerned there was absolutely nothing scientific about kick-starting a Harley Davidson. There was just one simple lesson to learn: If you don't kick it until it starts, you're not going for a ride! And that's how you start your success in this business.

Jeff Roberti

*"If you've ever said, 'If I could I would,'
network marketing allows you to do it!"*
Jeff Roberti

Background: Food Service
Year started in networking industry: 1983

**I was a broke and dissatisfied waiter when I got into network
marketing.** I was 21 years old and a friend of mine told me
about an opportunity meeting in Sarasota, Florida. When I got
there, they discussed being in business for yourself, being your own
boss, earning what you are worth, becoming more, and so on. That
night I saw average people making above-average incomes and
thought this might be my chance.

I didn't want to work for a corporation and build someone else's
dreams. My goal was to become a millionaire, and I eventually did!
Within 12 months I had my income at $100,000 a month. In my
second year I was up to $300,000 a month. It has been a fairytale!

Most of my co-workers and friends laughed about it when I first
got involved. They laughed about the products, the industry, and at
me. My father thought it would be a good experience though.

My greatest obstacles were employing myself, staying focused,
having the discipline and commitment to certain work habits, and
not taking rejection personally. You need to keep swinging the bat.
If I talk to ten people in one day, maybe one says yes. I get paid for
talking to ten people, but the result is one yes. I never worry about
the ones I can't sell; I worry about the ones I can't see!

Another obstacle was when I started having success. When people start having success they sometimes don't have the capacity to
handle it. Success is what you become as a person.

**The most fulfilling part of network marketing for me is the to-
tal financial independence.** What a thrill it is to be my own boss! But

equally fulfilling is having a product and an opportunity that touches and changes people's lives. I have over 100 people who I have helped earn over a million dollars in my organization, thousands of people who have earned a six-figure income, and tens of thousands of people who earn good income on a part-time basis. If you've ever said, "If I could I would," network marketing allows you to do it!

I have fulfilled my dreams with a beautiful home on the beach and the cars of my dreams. I even bought my mother a brand new car for Christmas. I put a big bow on it and handed her the keys. I have helped one of my brothers through college and another brother in getting a new home. It's wonderful being able to help others.

I retail and recruit all day long. That's my job! I start at 8 a.m. and work 'til I faint. I have an "all-out massive action" work ethic! When I am not on the phone, I am in front of a person. I could work 24 hours a day if I wanted to because of the different time zones in Europe and the Far East. I do a lot of conference calls and three-ways calls. Technology really helps. Then I go out on the road to do trainings and meetings. I like to get into the trenches.

My first year I spoke to over 10,000 people and was averaging 20 to 30 contacts a day. I was a recruiting machine! I talked with everybody who got within three feet of me. I went through a lot of noes, but I wouldn't buy other people's stories that weren't positive or receptive to my opportunity.

Eventually I would like to recruit everyone on the planet to use the product! When I learned about the company's product line at that first meeting, they mesmerized me. It is of the utmost importance to have conviction and enthusiasm when it comes to the products you promote.

There is no one surefire way to prospect people in network marketing. I teach that concepts are constant, but techniques can always vary. Audio tapes, coffee shops, satellite hookups, and videotapes are all different tools and techniques. The concept, and what you get paid for in this business, is talking to people. How you do that is up to you.

Personally, I give my prospects audio tapes to listen to that are developed by experts on nutrition, and then I follow up with them.

But you can run ads, talk to people on the street, use other people's warm market, or use people's living rooms—as long as you are talking to people and telling your company's story.

We get paid when we talk to people, and it's not that difficult. I feel the best way to recruit is the warm market. People are most comfortable with those they know, like, and trust.

Very often, your retail customers become your best distributors. My concept here is "retail to recruit." You show the product and you follow up. When you do, three things can happen: You get a steady customer, you get referrals, or they become one of your best distributors. Pretty simple isn't it?

Consistency and commitment are the keys to success in network marketing. You need consistency in your effort, work habits, and attitude. Have discipline and stay focused. But most of all, lead by example. You need to practice what you preach to your distributors.

The number one reason why people quit this industry is because they listen to those who know little or nothing about it and buy *their* story. When they get noes from some of their friends and family, they get negative instead of standing up for themselves and having belief.

Winners don't give up; they get up. My sponsor quit during my first month in the business. I had no education or experience, and my sponsor quit! But I still made it happen. I didn't use those things as excuses. I learned that if it is to be, it's up to me!

To really make your business explode, work on yourself more than your products and plan. How do you feel about you? Until you realize what you want and what you're capable of, you won't work your business with any purpose. Find out what makes you tick, then give it all you've got. Look for people who have a desire for more in life, a willingness to work, and are teachable! Then help them succeed.

Jan Ruhe

"There is a day that you get into network marketing, but nothing happens until the day network marketing gets into you."
Jan Ruhe

Background: Homemaker
Year started in networking industry: 1980

After I had my first child, Sarah, I made a decision to be a stay-at-home mom. One day a friend invited me to a skincare party down the street. I went, and when the party was over the hostess booked a future party with me in my home. When my party was over, she turned to me and said the words that literally changed my life: "You seem to be a wonderful hostess. I bet you would be great at selling this product." At that moment I was blown away because for so many years no one had said anything really positive to me. I got so excited that I signed up on the spot. I was 26 years old and decided I was going to be her top sales rep.

I went to a training the next week and it scared me to death! There was too much information and too much to learn. And even though I felt intimidated, I decided to give it my best shot and off into network marketing I went. But I fell flat on my face! I just couldn't sell the product. The only person who bought something from me was my grandmother. I was so discouraged and sad that I quit.

I then had another child, a son, Clayton, and during the next few years my marriage began to fall apart. As I watched it unravel, I began to think to myself, "How will my children and I survive?" I had to do something because I knew my marriage was going to end. As fate would have it, I was again invited to another home party, and this time it was for the company I'm with now.

165

From the moment I saw the product line, I decided to go for it. And that's the main reason why I've chosen to stay with this company for twenty years. For me, it's critical that I believe in a product before I can sell it. For others, I don't know if that's necessary.

I joined in March of 1980, and I remember on that day thinking I was going to succeed, no matter what, because my children were counting on me. Unfortunately, my sponsor quit shortly after I joined and she told me to stop calling her for support! I also found out I was pregnant again. At this point I had a 4-year-old, a 2-year-old, and a baby on the way.

A very serious future was unfolding for me, but this was the first time in my life where I actually felt hope. Watching my marriage crumble, and not having a real sense of where my children and I would end up, had left me feeling so hope-*less* for so long. But I suddenly found myself enthusiastic and courageous, and very excited about the possibilities before us.

It took me about five years to build a fairly solid downline. Was I discouraged? Yes. But I knew I could make it happen if I just didn't let up. Most of my friends were not supportive in any way, shape or form, so I turned it around on them. I felt that if they didn't want to support me, then they really weren't my friends. So I dropped them before they could drop me! People can label themselves as friends, but if they don't want to help you succeed beyond your wildest expectations, then are they really true friends? I cut many people out of my life back then, and you know what? Today I can't even remember their names!

When I first started my network marketing business, I put in anywhere from 10 to 50 hours a week. Today I work it only 2 hours a day, but my business has branched out into other areas of interest. I am an author of two books and working on a third. I am also a professional speaker for companies around the globe. How I spend my time is precious to me and I do my best to make every minute count. But I also make sure I find the time for fun stuff like river rafting, hiking, and cross-country skiing!

I truly am the most blessed woman in the world. Network marketing has created an incredible lifestyle for my children and

Bill, my wonderful husband of ten years. I have traveled and made friends all around the world, and I'm helping the leaders in my organization design their lives. My home is on top of a mountain in the western U.S., and the views are stunning. There's nothing like living on a mountaintop! I will be forever grateful for what network marketing has afforded me.

Although I consider everyone a potential recruit, I built my business by finding peak performers. My leaders are the ones who have lifted me up on their shoulders. Without them I could not have become the woman I am. I consider my leaders to be some of the best in the world. They know I am accessible to them whenever they need me, but they have also become very independent in their own right. In network marketing you'll find that the people who succeed and become leaders are generally self-motivated.

The whole key to network marketing is to build leaders and make them successful. Always be building two to three leaders and do whatever it takes to cultivate those relationships. Stop thinking about yourself and make *them* successful. Always be there to reach down, pick them up, and try again.

Meetings and events are a great way to keep your leaders on track. In addition to home meetings, we use a combination of weekly, monthly and national meetings to keep people plugged in. But I tell my leaders to be careful when it comes to guidance. By this I mean they should listen only to the people who are living the lifestyle they want to lead.

When it comes to recruiting, I think to myself, "Two friends a day brings freedom my way." I'm always looking for two people to prospect each and every day... *no less.* For me this is a realistic goal and I think it's realistic for most people. The fact is if you are consistent with your prospecting, you will build your business.

As for rejection, I have a "Who cares?" attitude. How many baskets do you think Michael Jordan missed? How many home runs has Mark McGwire missed? *Who cares?* The point is, all their hard work paid off! Don't let the people who reject you get inside your head and turn off your success switch.

There is a day that you get into network marketing, but nothing happens until the day network marketing gets into you. Until you get committed to your own desires and dreams, you aren't going anywhere in this industry. *Quitters never win and winners never quit!* You either jump on the ship or watch it sail by!

Just know, up-front, you will make many mistakes and have to hang in there. No one's perfect! One time I was introduced on stage as the top promoter of leaders in my company, and when I walked out on stage I realized I had two different shoes on! You need to loosen up and laugh in this industry!

If you are just getting involved in network marketing, take the advice of Winston Churchill who said, "Never, never, never quit!" Then ponder over these 5 "Ruhe-isms":

Ruhe-ism #1: There are no statues erected to remember the critics.

Ruhe-ism #2: Treat everyone as you would like them to treat your mother.

Ruhe-ism #3: Turn the corners of your mouth up at least once a day.

Ruhe-ism #4: Be so busy giving recognition that you don't need it.

Ruhe-ism #5: The greatest of all these is love!

Cindy Samuelson

"Network marketing is the key out of jail so you can work at home!"
Cindy Samuelson

Background: Sales
Year started in networking industry: 1988

I was born in a third world country, immigrated to America when I was young, and raised in poverty. I have always believed that I would succeed in life because I lived in America. My husband and I were well on our way to being millionaires before my 30th birthday. But a month before I was introduced to network marketing, we had just lost a half a million dollars in a business deal. We were devastated and way past broke!

The turning point in my life was the day I met a 23-year-old former bellman who had grown up with my daughter-in-law. He was using a nutritional supplement that improved his family's health and also generated an income. He went from earning $2 an hour to $15,000 per month—in less than two years! I had used the product myself, with instant results, so I agreed to meet with him about the opportunity. It was an eye-opening experience.

After I decided to become a distributor, I set tremendous goals for myself because this young man proved to me that it was possible. It took three years to earn a six-figure income and to become debt free again. It took nine years to earn $50,000 per month (I thought it would take two!).

My husband had 21 years of experience in corporate America, and he was very skeptical of what I was doing. Normally very supportive of me, he remained uncharacteristically quiet, if not inwardly angry, over my new venture. Only when my royalty checks went over $5,000 did he finally have a spark of interest!

I've learned nutritional products are the only ones I wish to promote in network marketing. If your mother takes my product and it helps her arthritis, she'll love it forever, and so will you! Because people get emotional about their experiences with nutritional products, I really don't have to sell them. They magically sell themselves.

In the beginning of my network marketing career, I stood in the way of my own success. I was very uncoachable. It took me two years to accept the fact I even needed a coach. I was self-centered and demanding of others. Fortunately, when I was ready, the coaches were there. I had good communication skills but not good leadership or people management skills. I had constant financial struggles the first two years because of these shortcomings. My coaches helped me address and correct these flaws. Because of that, I'll always devote time to personal development. The dividends are enormous!

The ability to make significant money brought me into network marketing. And with hard work, and the help of the money, my husband and I were able to salvage everything—our marriage, our family, and our finances.

But money isn't the only thing that excites me about our industry. What drives me today is seeing the hope in people's eyes and teaching others that the American dream is still very much alive. People are tired of traditional business and (rightly) believe it provides them no security. Network marketing is the key out of jail so you can work at home!

Working at home is truly a joy. I love the casual dress I never got to experience in the workplace. Now I only "dress up" for corporate functions! I spend 50 percent of my time on the telephone, and the other 50 percent I'm consistently doing one-on-one meetings, home opportunity meetings, and public opportunity meetings.

I use the Franklin Covey time management systems, but I don't busy myself with paperwork. I believe I'm only working when I'm with people. I make an effort to work every day but Sunday. I also think it's important to spend your life doing things that don't feel like work, like network marketing is for me. Technology has allowed me to stay at home and conduct my business. I do quite a bit of traveling, but my priorities are to be here at home. I often plan my trips around family fun so we can go together.

The first two years, it took a lot of effort and I put in all the time I possibly could into building my business. I had an agreement with my family that if they would allow me the freedom to work, we would take a whole summer off. After two years I had accomplished my goals, so we packed up for a summer long vacation to exotic locations around the world.

When prospecting, I don't spend my time with people who barely fog a mirror! I don't grovel and beg people to come to meetings. I look for people who have a desire to work and change their lives. I recruit people who are more successful and hungrier than me. When I was new to the business I used my upline for credibility to help me recruit good people.

I don't believe in the three-foot rule. I believe this opportunity can change people's lives but I don't try to convince someone who's unwilling to change themselves. I won't spend my time convincing a stranger, who just sneaked in from having a cigarette, to come to a meeting. I set high standards and use a prospect information sheet to find out exactly what the person wants. If there's someone I would really like to talk to about the business, I tailor the approach to them and their circumstances.

For example, if I'm talking to a mom and she asks what I do, I would say, "I teach women how to become financially independent while working at home spending time with their kids." I wear my "mom's hat" for that person. Last week I did a conference call with a former president of a major Fortune 500 company. It was important I speak with him like one executive to another. My "mom hat" wouldn't have worked with him but my "CEO hat" did. We need to learn to relate to people and help them look at how our industry will benefit their lives. The CEO wanted more time with his wife and could see our industry offered lifestyle. Today he's doing network marketing full-time!

Over the years I have learned to not take rejection personally. Who cares! I choose to surround myself with quality people. You can only become a giant in this industry one of two ways: you can surround yourself with dwarfs—not in stature, mind you, but in spirit— or you can surround yourself with giants. It's giants for me!

I go all-out in my business. That means I give it everything I've got energy-wise. When you're around me you're either going to catch on fire or you're going to melt! I never surround myself with whiners, moaners, and complainers. You're either part of the solution or you're part of the problem. If you're part of the solution then you're in the game. If you're in the game, you W-O-R-K! My mentor taught me the "Wealth Formula," which says you can't get rich only working 40 hours a week, so I work hard and consistently.

Another important lesson I learned is this: Having fun is vital. When it comes to what I do for a living, I've never had such fun in my entire life! I've learned to be in control of my personal disciplines. When you're in control of your life, it's easy to have fun. And what could be more fun than helping people?

There's only one reason why people don't succeed in network marketing: they don't believe in the magnitude of the opportunity or in their ability to succeed. It's exactly the same thing as Roger Banister breaking the four-minute mile. Once he broke the "barrier," other people believed they could do it too! A lot of people don't believe it's possible for them to succeed in this industry. That's where they can use other people's examples. If I can do it, you can do it too!

Commitment and perseverance are vital to your success. Never, never, never give up!

DREAM ACHIEVERS

FACTOID
#7

When asked if they approach everyone
when prospecting, or are selective:

69%   Everyone

31%   Selective

Dave and Beverly Savula

"There are prospects everywhere who desperately need an opportunity, and getting to them is our only passion!"
Dave Savula

Interview conducted with Dave only.
Background: Student
Year started in networking industry: 1966

My goal in network marketing was to create a six-figure income. But today I make seven figures! I was 18 years old and in college when a friend introduced me to network marketing. I was very impressed with the potential income and lifestyle it could provide. Years later, my career led me to the legal service industry where I found a unique company that was leading the charge to help consumers. I didn't hesitate to work it full-time and it has become a massive income opportunity.

I've always had a very positive attitude and, because of that, I have always believed I was a winner. If I had doubts, it was about the industry. But I never had self-doubt. Both Beverly and I grew up on the same street. We come from the same mindset and have the same positive attitude. If anything, our only obstacle is the fact that there are prospects everywhere who desperately need an opportunity and getting to them is our only passion.

This is the only industry where you must help other people succeed in order to succeed yourself. I am thankful I can share an opportunity with people that can radically change their lives. And, in over 30 years, this industry has given me the chance to help many of the leaders in my organization earn six-figure incomes.

I attribute my accomplishments to a great work ethic and the system I've had in place for many years. I have intense weeks and relaxed weeks. The intense ones consist of giving opportunity seminars every day, from Monday through Friday, while a typical day is spent working with my organization.

When I was new to the business, I committed to doing two presentations a day, in addition to a weekly meeting. The presentations were only 15 to 20 minutes long so they could be done in the morning, during lunch, and after work.

People say I'm a great motivator, which I do simply by telling the truth about network marketing. I then combine that with the truth of the legal industry, which used to be a luxury, but now is a necessity. I deliver the facts about our program which, in and of themselves, are great motivators.

Not everyone is a potential recruit for me, but everyone could potentially lead me to somebody who would be interested. I may go after a person because I am trying to get to someone he or she knows. The first thing I look for is somebody who has done presentations which, of course, includes everybody in sales. Second, I look for people who have a considerable source of influence and a good warm market. I then endeavor to develop them so that, within three weeks, they are up and running on their own. Prospects are everywhere; you just need to keep your eyes open.

I have the most foolproof three-step approach in the world when I present to someone. First is "Show," second is "15 Minutes," and third is "You may or may not be interested." It doesn't matter how you say it, it all sounds the same. For example, "I have something I want to show you. It will only take 15 minutes. And, by the way, you may or may not be interested." Or you can say, "Let me stop by for 15 minutes. I have something I want to show you. By the way, you may or may not be interested." You can put it in any order, but either way it comes out the same. The key word is "show." That's pretty duplicatable, isn't it?

The main key to success in network marketing is duplication. My presentation needs to be done exactly the same every single time. The baseball field never changes but the spectators do!

You also need commitment, and to treat the business like a business. If someone isn't interested in my opportunity, he or she does not understand it. I just don't deal with their rejection. I'm on a mission to find people who *do* understand it!

Facts, not hype, keep people in the business. Most people quit because they weren't properly informed on how network marketing

175

works. You need to know a lot about the company you're joining. You need to find a company where their product or service has a market niche, and a compensation program that rewards you for moving that product or service and sponsoring.

Focus on where you're going, and don't look back! Don't let the lions eat you. In the Bible you'll find the story of Daniel in the lion's den. He focused on his faith and belief, not the lions. Don't let the lions in your life change your focus or direction.

Goals—there is a misconception in goal-setting. Some people tell you to set long-term goals; some tell you to set short-term goals. The only goals you really need to set are day to day. This is how you build a successful network marketing company. Now go do it!

Erling J. Schroeder

"There was no doubt in my mind that I was going to be successful."
Erling J. Schroeder

Background: Restaurant Owner
Year started in networking industry: 1983

Before network marketing, I owned and operated three restaurants for 17 years. I had an employee who embezzled a lot of money from me and I lost everything. I was 53 and had nowhere to go. I had to live with my mother because I couldn't afford rent, and I was constantly looking over my shoulder to see if they were going to turn off my phone or take away my car. I happened to take a look at a network marketing opportunity and in three months I had made a substantial amount of money. In one year I was making a six-figure income!

When I first got involved in my company, most everyone around me was saying, "What's he up to now?" But my sister and my mother came to my support rather quickly by getting on the products and experiencing great results. And even though most everyone in the family recognizes my success, many of them still haven't gotten involved in the business.

When I have a strong belief in something, I can accomplish it. In the restaurant business, I expanded from a "hole in the wall" to three big restaurants with 300 employees. Many other things in my life have been the same way. However, I've had some negative experiences in other network marketing companies in the past, and, if anything, at first that's what gave me a little doubt. But once I learned all about my company and the vision they had, I knew I was really onto something. There was no doubt in my mind I was going to be successful.

The most frustrating obstacle for me was finding people who realized my business opportunity was legitimate—not a "get-

rich-quick" scam. Our society is living on the edge of what is called a "cream puff attitude." It means we want "it" today, and if we don't get it today we quit and do something else. My biggest challenge was being able to communicate the commitment level it takes to be successful in this business. Many people just didn't want to put in the time and effort to make their businesses work.

I get up early every day to work my business. The first thing I do is my exercises. About three days a week I go to the driving range and hit golf balls for about 45 minutes. After that I sit down and organize my day, and usually do a little reading, either spiritual or self-help oriented. I then figure out who I'm calling and where I'm going.

I do a lot of telephone work and meet people for one-on-one presentations, either at restaurants or in their homes. We also do two meetings a month. In the evening I do three-way calls with my distributors for their prospects, winding down around 10 p.m.

Recently, I have slowed down my pace a bit. When I first got started in network marketing, I worked anywhere from 60 to 80 hours a week. Today it's 30 to 40. Now that I can pull back some, I do things I never dreamed of doing six or seven years ago when I was very aggressively building my business. I play a lot of golf and I enjoy my home. I guess I'm "smelling the roses" now! And I take comfort in knowing that when I'm gone I have made a contribution to the world during my time here. The money is great, but being able to touch people's lives is what it's all about for me.

What I wanted most of all was freedom. I was under so much stress with bill collectors during those tough restaurant years that I would have done anything to erase that out of my life. And believe me, it's now all erased!

I want to savor and enjoy the success my network marketing business has given me. I may choose to go into a retirement phase soon and spend more time doing some things I've always wanted to do. But I will always keep my finger in the business helping my people reach their goals.

Motivating a downline is almost an impossibility. You can't get people to do what you want them to do, unless it is what *they* want to do. People are willing to do only what they really want to do. Motivation is a byproduct of a burning desire, and that's up to each individual to create. The best way I have found to motivate them, even just a little, is to keep painting the picture of the end result. They need to feel compelled to keep doing the nuts and bolts of the business on a daily basis. That only works for the short term though. Your job as a network marketer isn't to motivate people; it's to support and guide them when they need help.

I take advantage of every opportunity to talk to others about my company's products and business opportunity. I don't discriminate against anyone. I just talk to people and that always leads me to where I want to go.

When I recruit someone into the business, I develop rapport initially and build a bridge so they start asking me what I do. When they ask, I say I'm in the wellness industry and that we have a very unique program that helps people with their health challenges. And then I'll add that I help people set themselves up in home-based businesses with our company, its products, and the opportunity. After I say that, they are always interested in at least hearing about our products.

When I first got in the industry I let rejection become a personal thing, especially when close friends and relatives responded negatively. I learned early on that this is a numbers game, and that if they rejected the opportunity, they weren't rejecting me.

My job was to keep telling people about it until I got a yes. To say that rejection doesn't bother me today would be a lie. But rather than letting rejection bother me for a day or week, it bothers me for less than a minute now!

I have developed ten steps to keep my business simple and duplicatable:

1. Don't become a victim of "Analysis Paralysis." Make sure you're working your business every single day. Just do it!
2. Learn to use your company's tools. Not taking full advantage of all the training and sales aids your company offers would be equivalent to building a house without availing yourself of the modern power tools of the trade.
3. Don't keep reinventing the wheel. Be sure your company has a simple, duplicatable system that is time tested and has made money for a lot of people. Just plug into that system and work it every single day.

4. If your company sells nutritional products, don't try to become a nutrition expert. Learn the basics of each product, but don't get overly technical.
5. Keep product follow-up simple but consistent. Don't get too personal. Stay focused on the products, their potential benefits and how to use them consistently and correctly.
6. Develop a simple game plan for yourself and your new consultants. The key to success is to establish a pattern of daily activities that need to be done over and over for an extended period of time.
7. Lead with the product and mission first, then follow up with the opportunity. You need to generate an interest in your company's products before your talk about the money that can be made as a representative. If you do it the other way around, you run the risk of your prospects looking at your company as one of those "pyramid schemes."
8. Make a major issue out of the first 90 days for new consultants. If you don't do this, you will constantly be re-building your organization due to attrition. Most people fail in network marketing because they didn't have proper training and guidance during the first 90 days. So make sure you give your downline the support they need during this time.
9. Don't overwhelm a new consultant. You can scare them with too much training too soon. Keep it simple so they see themselves training other people. Remember, what you do with them is what they will expect to do with their recruits.
10. Go out and have fun! Having fun means keeping the business simple. Simple means duplicatable, and a duplicatable system ensures the success of your organization.

Having fun is probably the most important ingredient to making network marketing work. I think a lot of people are under the impression that network marketing *isn't* fun but, the truth is, it's full of laughs and surprises!

For example, two business partners of mine and I, all of whom had been in the business for only about 30 days, were going on a trip in a van. We had left Lincoln, Nebraska at around midnight and were headed for Denver, about 500 miles away. We were all tired from doing meetings all day and night, and now it was late and we were off for an all-night road trip to do even more meetings the next day.

It was my turn to drive. Along the way, slumber overtook me and the van started veering off the road. Fortunately I hit a mile marker which woke me up, along with everyone else. We were able to stop and no one got hurt. But there were a few minutes there that were really scary. As we all calmed down, my sponsor said in a heavy southern accent, "Boy, you about wiped out three budding millionaires!" His words could not have been more truly spoken!

It's sad to see new distributors quit the business without giving it some honest effort. They fail because they're looking for instant gratification. Many people get into this industry and think that in 30 days they're going to be rich. They need to realize that building a foundation is essential before they build a whole house. Their first few years in network marketing are that foundation phase. Unfortunately, that's when most people give up.

I always tell people, "Understand that in the first six months you will be severely underpaid for your effort and commitment. But when you get through that phase, you'll eventually be saying, 'Wow, I'm getting paid a lot more than I ever thought!'"

My advice to anyone who is just starting in network marketing is to understand the *potential* of this industry. Second, find a great company that has competent leadership, the best products and a lucrative compensation plan. Third, realize that if anyone can do it, so can you.

Finally, be focused and committed to a plan, and work it over and over and over again—every single day—until it does what you want it to do. Along the way, be sure to read inspirational books to stay motivated and, above all else—never, never give up!

Tom and Linda Shea

"If every brand new network marketer could somehow swap places with us and experience the lifestyle we have now, everyone in the world would eventually be doing network marketing!"
Tom and Linda Shea

Background: Government, Business Owner
Year started in networking industry: 1989

Q: What did you do before network marketing?
Linda: I owned a large hair salon for 18 years.
Tom: I was an Assistant Director of Contracts and Procurement for the Palm Beach County Government for 22 years.

Q: How did you get introduced to the company you're now with?
Linda: Working in a salon put me in contact with a lot of people. I always had a lot of customers bringing information in with them on various network marketing companies. My sister was my partner in the salon and someone had introduced her to the products. Frankly, I was not too enchanted with the idea. Now I know it was because I didn't understand it. But, regardless, I fell in love with the products. Then, as time went on, my sister started to do well with the business. Out of fear of loss I decided to join too. Tom really didn't want to get involved—that is, until he saw my check in the third month. Then he said, "You might want to add my name to your contract!"

Q: Did the product quality influence your decision to join your company?
Tom: Yes. Viable products are what govern long-term success in this industry.
Linda: My experience with network marketing is that 99 percent of the people I work with aren't salespeople. The products have to be so good that people simply want to tell others about them. You need to be very excited about what you represent before others can get enthusiastic too.

Q: Were your family and friends supportive of your decision to start a network marketing business?

Linda: Most of our friends laughed at us!

Tom: But our family *was* very supportive. Our four kids realized we were on a mission to change our lives, as we needed to. After all, three of them were in college and one was traveling abroad! So, financially, we had to be very sure what we were getting involved in wasn't some fly-by-night thing that was going to be gone tomorrow.

Linda: Our kids were our very best support. They wanted us to succeed!

Q: Did you ever have self-doubt?

Tom: That's natural for everyone in this business. If people tell you they don't have self-doubt, they're probably not telling the truth! But once you see your organization maturing, the success comes easier. You can see it working and your belief level rises.

Linda: Our standard joke is "Neither of us quit on the same day." If one is down the other is up, and that's why we're still here!

Q: What was your driving motivation to succeed in network marketing?

Tom: I came from an upper-level government background. It was a very regimented, rigid structure. I was tired of the politics and, after 22 years, I felt I had given enough to public service! So now it was time to change direction and get out of it.

Linda: I wanted more choices in my life. If I didn't want to work on Christmas Eve, I didn't want to have to. When I owned that hair salon, it really owned me. I wanted to be able to pick and choose who I worked with and also the hours I worked. Today we have choices that we didn't have before.

Q: Do you feel you've reached your goals?

Tom: So far our goals have given us the quality of life we've always wanted.

Linda: Absolutely! But we are always challenging ourselves with new goals.

Q: What were your greatest obstacles in succeeding?

Linda: Mine was myself. I didn't consider myself a salesperson, but I hung in there because I loved our products. Since I was an introvert and shy, it was hard for me to break out of that mold and approach people or speak in front of groups. But in that third month I got a wonderful check and thought to myself, "I'll *learn* to speak! I'll figure this business out!" I realized that in order to be successful I had to do what I had to do.

Tom: I didn't like to speak in front of people either. However, I kept looking at the bigger picture and understood that if I just kept doing what I was supposed to be doing, I would get to where I wanted to go.

Q: What is the most fulfilling part of network marketing for you?

Linda: If I had to pick one thing, it would be helping other people succeed.

Tom: The philosophy in network marketing is you become successful only if you help other people. With that in mind, it's a win-win situation.

Q: Could you describe a typical week?

Tom: In the beginning we spent 75 to 80 percent of our time recruiting. We still recruit today. But now that our organization has matured, we spend most of our time supporting them. We do three-way calls, conference calls, traveling to speak at meetings—that sort of thing.

Linda: When we first started, ten years ago, we were very excited because we saw that light at the end of the tunnel. We talked to everyone, worked 16-hour days and our organization grew rapidly. But today we don't need to work as hard because we have security. We have income that comes in every single month—whether we lift a finger or not. But we still choose to work because we love it and it's fun!

Q: Describe how you motivate your downline.

Tom: We supply validation for them. Our downline has seen us go from nothing to the highest possible rank in our company. Just our being there for them to talk to is proof network marketing works. They know we traveled the same road they're traveling, so it's motivating for them to know they're on the right track.

Q: Do you use meetings and events to grow your business?
Tom: Yes. Typically we do a weekly meeting and also a monthly training. The weekly meetings present the opportunity and the monthly trainings cover the how-to aspects.

Q: How do you deal with rejection?
Linda: When we first started, we took it personally. When our friends rejected us, it was difficult to accept. Today we still hate it, but we know it's a fixed thing we can't get rid of. Instead, I remind myself that what I have to offer people is a fantastic opportunity, and if they don't see what I see in my company, then shame on them! Look at what it did for us!
Tom: You develop a mind-set as time goes on. I realized that when people rejected me, they didn't add to my business but they didn't take anything away from it either. It's sort of a neutral feeling, but it's better than spending your energy getting upset about it!

Q: How many hours a week do you commit to your business?
Linda: Between 30 and 40. But then there are weeks we suffer withdrawal from our kids and we'll take a week off to visit them. That's what's wonderful about network marketing—the time freedom.

Q: What is your most effective approach when talking to people about your business opportunity?
Tom: In general, when you're in a conversation the best way is to wait for the question, "What do you do for a living?" From there it's an open door to talk about what we do. But most of all you need to become a good listener and find out what each person wants.

Q: Is everyone a potential recruit for you or do you look for a certain type of person?
Tom: In network marketing, you're searching for people who want the kind of life that you have. We always say we're "sick and tired of being sick and tired." Although we don't prejudge, we look for people who want our quality of life.
Linda: I only work with people I like! It's a privilege to hear about my business! If, after talking a bit, I don't like the person on the bus sitting next to me, I don't tell them about it.

Q: Do you have a funny experience to share?

Tom: We had an opportunity to introduce some people to our products during a large Sunday afternoon bingo game. One of our products is a face-lift product, and when it's applied the person has to lay down with their feet elevated. So we had these four ladies on the floor with their feet up in between the bingo games!

Linda: We're always telling our distributors that if you're not having fun, you're not doing this business right.

Q: What are the keys to success in network marketing?

Tom: You need persistence. It's a business that gets built over time, so you need to hang in there. Linda and I are two people you would have never thought would have gotten involved in network marketing. We both had solid jobs and a great income. But we also had goals beyond what that could provide, so we got involved in network marketing to achieve them. Even on our worst days we just kept moving forward because we knew what the payoff would be.

Linda: You also need goals. Goals will motivate you to get up and brush yourself off when you're going through the hard times. You need to be working *for* something in order to have a reason to go after it.

Q: Now that you've been successful in network marketing, what are your future plans?

Tom: We want to set up a financial future for our children. We also want to be able to help our distributors get to our level.

Linda: We want to continue to grow. Network marketing has treated us well and we enjoy what we do. We do it because it's fun and we'll continue to enjoy life and help people.

Tom: If every brand new network marketer could somehow swap places with us and experience the lifestyle we have now, everyone in the world would eventually be doing network marketing!

Q: Why do you think people quit network marketing?

Tom: People are conditioned for instant gratification. There's an old saying that says, "People don't fail at network marketing, they just quit."

Linda: And people simply can't handle the rejection. Their best friend says no and they're out of it. It's a shame because if you don't quit it will work.

Q: What advice could you give to people who are just getting involved in network marketing?

Tom: Commit your goals to paper! Write them down. When you do, they become more real to you. Then continue to forge ahead. And be sure to use the knowledge you can gain from the experience of your successful upline.

Linda: Just know that this a rollercoaster ride. You're likely to have a lot of downs, but you're also going to have wonderful ups. You'll find somebody who really wants to make it and you'll be helping them get there. There's no other feeling in the world like it. You'll be on an incredible high. But then tomorrow your best friend in the world may tell you you're crazy and you might want to quit. But when you have that goal in mind you'll know that the rollercoaster is going to go up again. So be smart and don't quit. Keep on going!

Eileen Silva

"I've learned far more from my failures than from my accidental successes."
Eileen Silva

Background: Education
Year started in networking industry: 1982

I had been diagnosed as incurably ill with a rare autoimmune disease and was searching for meaning in my life when I got involved in network marketing. Since the age of 27, I had been very sick and thought I was dying for about a decade. I had spent over $200,000 chasing relief with drugs and therapy, but I found nothing effective until I began to work with an immunologist by cleansing, balancing, and oxygenating. For over a decade now I haven't taken so much as a single aspirin or any allopathic medications whatsoever. My network marketing company's synergistic and cleansing emphasis in the product line made me realize I had to revamp my thinking about how to achieve maximum health and wellness. And I now teach integrative medicine to doctors and health professionals,

I was making over $100,000 in my spare time in network marketing before I ever quit my teaching job. In my highest-paid year as a schoolteacher, I had earned less than $40,000. With a current monthly income far in excess of annual teaching salary, I have to pinch myself when I think of how this incredible wealth has opened up time and income freedom options for us.

Believe it or not, it was an IRS (federal tax) audit that sparked my interest in network marketing. I was very upset because I had already paid over $10,000 in income tax, had all my receipts, and was honest in filling out the forms. The day I had the audit I was assessed almost a thousand dollars more in income tax for a disallowed "allowable" deduction; and when I got home that night the headline in the newspaper was, "Governor Ronald Reagan Pays Zero Income Tax!" I was livid!

About an hour later my brother arrived. He was a machinist at the time, and when I told him about the audit he said, "Well, I've got the answer...you need to get into a home-based business." And I said, "What do *you* know about them?" He told me he had joined a company that sold tennis shoes via mail order. I then decided to join his company because he told me that I could legally write off my trips to see the Atlanta Braves play baseball! I wasn't sure he knew what he was talking about, but for a $20 fee, I decided to take a chance—and I've never regretted it. Luckily, my family was very supportive of my starting my own business, and today they have lots of shoes to prove it!

Although the company went bankrupt about five months later, I consider that short adventure a turning point in my life. I enrolled 87 people, had a tremendous amount of fun, and realized that this type of work was something I could see myself doing. I just needed to learn how to make some money at it, since $347 was my biggest check with my first company.

I was originally sent to my current network marketing company as a "corporate spy." The company I was with at the time had hired me as a trainer, and they wanted me to find out why the other company was attracting so much attention in the industry.

I'm not a good spy and really didn't want to do it, but I ended up being talked into going. While on my spy visit to the company, I sampled every product and took them back home with me. Over the next few months I tested them on a lot of people and everyone loved them. Hands down, these products are what convinced me to join the company. I discovered a new phase of evolution in my understanding of health, and I saw a tremendous opportunity before me.

My greatest obstacle was self-sabotage. When I felt as though someone was working against me, I went to the closest mirror to see who it was. I was my own worst enemy. I realized my insecurities early on, so anytime I wanted to take my business to a new level, I took a long hard look inside myself. I still do that today.

My personal mission is to improve wellness in the world, including mental, physical, emotional, spiritual and financial wellness. Helping people achieve total wellness, or "body balance" as I like to refer to it, is my central driving force.

Network marketing has made me a totally independent businessperson. If I want to buy a new car, for example, I no longer think, "Can I afford a new car?" Instead, I just think "increase" and go make more money. That's the power of the entrepreneur, and it excites me to no end when I realize what's possible for all of us.

I've come so far since my school teaching days. My husband Taylor Hegan and I have estates in two lakeside communities in two different states, and we own other real estate. I have a staff of five employees including a maid who cooks my meals, brings me coffee in bed, gets my morning newspaper, and rolls down my shades at night. Today's lifestyle is pretty different than my "other" life.

I have also created a computer system called *Body System Profile* that is specifically designed to offer insights on cleansing, balancing, and oxygenating the body in the major system areas.

I've written books and training tapes, have my own radio show, and I'm a guest speaker on many other radio and TV shows. I also write business articles including my monthly magazine column called "Still Telling It Like It Is." It makes me feel good to know that I'm making a difference in the lives of so many people. I am thrilled that the more money I make, the more people it means I'm helping.

In fact, if it weren't for network marketing, I wouldn't have met my husband, Taylor. He was just a name on a prospect list that I had obtained. There were lots of names on the list and while on a tax write-off business trip, I just sat down and called each local person, one right after the other, looking for someone who would consider my business. When Taylor answered the phone, I gave him a little pitch on my business opportunity and he said, "I'd love to meet with you." I almost fainted because he was supposed to be this big-hitter in the industry. When I met with him, he ended up recruiting *me* into *his* business, and we starting working together. We launched a new weight-loss product in the U.S. and made over $21,000 our first month, even though the product turned out to be a great performance disappointment. It's a fluke that we ever met, but we eventually got married, and today we still make a great team and still work our business together.

I have done literally everything I've dreamed of doing, so now I have the mindset that I need to expand my thinking and keep creating more wonderful things in the lives of others. For me it's all about making a contribution to the world around me.

I conduct 95 percent of my business on the phone. In addition to the frequent 3-way calls I do with my leaders, I conduct a "Stay-at-Home Wealth Building Phone System" tele-conference three nights a week. One night a week I offer a business training call "Let's Get Started." On Wednesday nights I do a product training call. Then on Thursdays we have a 22-minute live presentation call where the leaders of the company present the business to new prospects as well as give a 20-minute weight-loss phone clinic. And then, of course, there're my Sunday night radio talk shows. So, I'm frequently on the phone!

I inspire my organization by helping them get their *why* in place. If I can get them to discover why they're in network marketing in the first place, their motivation can then come from within. The challenges of gaining self-confidence and finding enthusiasm then take care of themselves. I basically plug them into their own mission and help them design an appropriate business plan. My role is to promote the development of leaders, rather than to manage people.

I have a knack for engaging people in conversations, so I use that little talent as my best tool when prospecting. I don't go around *trying* to talk with everyone within three feet about network marketing, but it often just happens.

For example, when I'm on a plane I wear a button that advertises one of my products. It says, "Suddenly Slim...Ask me!" I will not say one word about that button unless someone asks me about it; when that happens, I develop a conversation with that person. I would, however, never approach an overweight person to talk to them about my weight loss products. I don't try to "fix" people.

In my experience, people will often ask me what I do when we are in a casual conversation. If that happens, I just say I am in the business of helping people balance their body chemistry, reverse the aging process, and take off weight without dieting. Invariably people say, "Oh my gosh, have I got to talk to you!"

When a prospects isn't receptive to the opportunity I'm offering, it's because the timing isn't right for them. I'm well aware that people live busy, complex lives. And fitting a new network marketing business in can sometimes be quite a challenge.

I won't waste my time trying to convince people who aren't ready to work hard and make it happen. I would much rather spend my time searching for the person who *is* ready to design a vision and make it a reality than trying to turn a plow horse into a thoroughbred. I also welcome product users who simply want to buy things at wholesale. They are the backbone of my check.

Don't expect to get lucky by sponsoring one person and then making millions. To make money in network marketing, you need to put in the same hard work as with any other new business venture. Any seasoned network marketer will tell you that you need to help your downline succeed in order for you to succeed. So don't think you're going to sign up and cash in with little or no work.

By the way, it's okay to fail, fail and fail again. There are precious lessons in failing, and I believe that my failures have proven both necessary and useful. I've learned far more from my failures than from my accidental successes.

Choose a sponsor the way you choose a spouse. They need to hold your hand and have high integrity. You *must* be able to trust them and they must be able to mentor you.

Once you have your sponsor in place, have a vision, focus on it, and be enthusiastic, persistent, and never quit! And once you've decided to embark on a network marketing business adventure, give yourself at least two years to learn the ropes.

Do yourself a favor. Learn all you can about the new industry you're in and realize it is evolving rapidly. If you are serious about succeeding in network marketing, you need to do the things that successful network marketers do! And the most important thing is to learn all you can about the industry. Network marketing looks deceptively easy but, like anything worthwhile, it requires effort.

Network marketing is one of the few level playing fields that I know of. Whether you are 18 or 80, male or female, able-bodied or handicapped, black or white or anything in between, you can become wealthy and free in this.

Just do whatever it takes and you *really can* have it all!

Todd Smith

"The mindset is what makes network marketing work."
Todd Smith

Background: Real Estate
Year started in networking industry: 1990

There came a time during my real estate career when I realized I no longer enjoyed what I was doing. Once I made the decision to get out of that industry, I began looking at my options. I had always wanted to be in business for myself; however, because I had no formal education I was not in a position to walk away from a $400,000 annual income.

I checked out franchising and other business opportunities. When I studied the requirements and the risks involved with those companies, I was confident I could make any of them work. But I also knew that, in the long-run, I would end up right back in my current situation. Although I would be making a significant income, I would have little time freedom and I wouldn't find the quality of life I was seeking.

One day I was listening to Brian Tracy's cassette series, *Getting Rich in America*, where he was talking about starting your own business. He said that 85 percent of what you need to know to run a successful business could be learned from building a network marketing organization. Until that time I had always had a negative attitude about network marketing, but I decided to research the possibilities.

I answered an ad and made a phone call. The gentleman told me he was making $40,000 a month. If I was interested, I would need to meet with him so he could show me how to do the same thing. I met him the next week and became a distributor in a company selling nutritional and skincare products. Within four months I built a downline of almost 2,000 distributors. In fact, I set some income records that, to this day, I believe have not yet been broken.

I spent a year in that company but soon felt their compensation plan made it difficult for the part-time person to succeed. Because of that, as well as a few other policies and procedures I didn't like, I started to lose belief in the company. That's when I started looking for other opportunities.

Using a specific criteria, I examined over a hundred different network marketing opportunities. One day I got a call from a gentleman who was a distributor of the company I'm now with. After taking a close look at the company and their management team, I decided to get involved.

The products did influence my decision, but I was impressed with the company's opportunity more than anything else. I looked at the business side of it first and then examined the products. They had to be consumables which were in demand—products that people needed and used—and priced fairly. They also needed to represent large and growing markets, not some fly-by-night product that was going to come and go.

In my first month I showed 80 people the plan and sponsored 20. That generated a significant first paycheck. From there my checks doubled and tripled. Now, seven years later, my annual income is over $2 million and it keeps growing!

I've always had the desire to create financial security in my life. I wanted to reach a level where I could make enough money to provide well for my family and maintain a quality lifestyle. I wanted to able to spend more time with my wife and children. I have earned over $8 million in seven years, so I guess I'm on my way!

Everybody close to me was supportive. They believed in me and, I'm happy to say, I never had any dreamstealers. But to date I have had only one family member and one friend working the business with me. Everyone else said no!

I never had any self-doubt, but I've had many frustrating "down days." Everyone in our industry experiences those challenging and sometimes depressing days. If you get discouraged it's hard to stay focused and excited. So many people fail because they don't continue to do what they need to do day-in and day-out. But I would keep going and working towards my goals, even when I felt discouraged.

On weekdays I get up every morning about 8:30, have coffee with my wife and spend time with my four kids. Then I get to work and I'm busy until dinnertime. I spend most of my day on the phone doing three-way calls helping my key distributors. From 5 p.m. to 8:30 p.m., I have dinner and spend more time with my wife and kids. Then I go back up to my office and answer voicemail messages, do more three-way calls, and conduct conference calls for groups. On Fridays I work until 5 p.m. because my wife and I use Friday nights to go out on a date. On Saturdays I work only until 2 p.m. And I don't start working again until Sunday evening about 9:30 p.m., after the kids have gone to bed. I also travel six days a month conducting presentations and training sessions for large groups. And I usually hit 12 cities in those six days.

I do a lot of meetings, but I don't consider myself a motivating person. I encourage my distributors by working with them to find out where the breakdowns in their businesses are and then helping them fix those problem areas. I also help them identify their goals and their reasons for working their businesses. Plus, I keep in close communication with them through the company's voicemail system. I have also developed a system that the entire company uses as a training foundation. And my downline can access that information on cassettes.

When I recruit, I am selective. I look for people who are at a point in their lives where they're considering other career opportunities or want to diversify. I want partners with strong character and integrity who will follow through on their commitments.

My best approach is to have my guests listen in on a national telephone conference call, or I give them a tape to play. I believe these two approaches are efficient ways to share the business because I don't have the time to drive across town to pick people up and take them to meetings!

After they listen to the call or tape, and are still interested, that's when I meet with them. We talk about the direction they want to go in life and I answer their questions.

Rejection is never something I take to heart. As a real estate agent I made hundreds of sales calls a week. I'm numb to rejection. No doesn't mean personal rejection, it just means the prospect isn't interested in what you have to offer. If a waitress goes around a restaurant asking people if they want coffee and most of them say no, she's not going to go into the back room and cry, is she? If they say no, I treat them with respect, thank them for their time, and never take it personally. And I go on to the next person.

One of the greatest keys to success is to know what your desire in life is, and then have the discipline to do the things you know you need to do, every day, all day, even when you don't feel like doing them. There's no two ways about it, you've got to have the desire to succeed. If you don't, you'll get discouraged when the first person says no, and you may quit. Your passion for success is the only thing that gives you the willpower and determination to keep going. This mindset is what makes network marketing work. It's not complicated. There are certain fundamental activities that, when done over and over, day after day, will lead you to success.

Many new distributors become discouraged and quit within the first 72 hours. Unfortunately, family members who try to steal their dreams often cause their discouragement. Or, when their five best friends don't get as excited about the business as they are, they end up doubting their own ability to make a decision and look for others to validate it. When it isn't validated, they quit.

People also quit because they don't get out of their comfort zones. What I mean is they develop a tremendous fear of the telephone and what might happen if they pick it up, call someone and the voice on the other end says no. They just don't have the courage or the discipline to make the necessary prospecting calls. They end up saying network marketing isn't for them, but that's just an excuse because almost anyone can make a phone call!

There are four things you need to do to succeed in network marketing. First, determine what you really want out of your business and put your goals in writing. Second, ask somebody in your upline whom you admire to help you put together a business plan. Third, get focused and work that plan. Remember, like any business, it's going to take time to develop. Understand that the rewards that will follow your discipline will be greater in network marketing than in any other business. And finally, don't let anyone discourage you!

DREAM ACHIEVERS

FACTOID
#8

When asked if they had self-doubt when
starting their network marketing businesses:

49% Yes

51% No

Carolyn Spargur

*"You can make money or you can make
excuses, but you can't make both!"*
Carolyn Spargur

Background: Food Service, Secretarial
Year started in networking industry: 1966

Thank God network marketing came along when it did. I shudder to think where my life would be if it hadn't. Before network marketing, I worked for an attorney during the day. And at night I was a hostess in a big restaurant. I was raising four children alone, and I took that job when one of them needed braces.

When I was working in the office, I knew a hospital administrator who was making a good salary. (We did the payroll for the hospital.) I was working hard for $350 a week, and her check was over $1,000. She approached me one day and offered to let me try a cleaning product. It rode around in the back of my car for about a month until I moved into a dirty place that needed to be cleaned! I remember she said it would do everything. So, I cleaned all my dirty furniture, my bathtub—*everything*. And she was absolutely right. I got really excited!

Because of that product, which got me interested, I signed up right away. I continued using the product and everyone kept encouraging me to sponsor. But I didn't want any part of sponsoring —I simply didn't like selling. Eventually, however, they convinced me to start sponsoring. They told me that would enable me to get the product at a discount and earn money to pay for the gasoline I was using while driving around showing it to all of my friends. And that made sense to me.

Then one of my more intelligent girlfriends, who was cleaning with it in a hospital, asked me what was in it and if it was safe. So I called my upline to ask and he said, "Why don't you come to a presentation tonight and find out?" So I went. At that meeting they also talked about food supplements, which really interested me too. My daughter had been born with a physical challenge and I had two asthmatic sons. It made sense to me that if you give the body what it needs, it can heal itself.

When I got involved with the nutritional products, I set out to save the world and got crazy about the opportunity! I'd give my friends products to take, whether they liked it or not, because I loved them. I just wouldn't take no for an answer! Fortunately, I have been blessed with good friends who have always supported me. They knew me and that I was honest and excited which, in turn, got them excited.

I love helping people. When I meet someone new, I know exactly how network marketing can help them. Every time I look into someone's eyes and they say, "I think I can do this," I say, "I know you can do this." Sometimes I get more excited than they do!

I never had self-doubt. I am so determined. When I believe in something, I fight for it and have no fear.

If anything, time is my only obstacle! I just mailed 32 boxes of new information to my sales leaders to keep them up-to-date, and it took a lot of time. When you enjoy what you're doing and gain momentum, everything rolls like a snowball. And it is truly a labor of love!

I am very much into attitude and help my downline gear their attitudes toward success. I like to make sure they know how to teach our career plan and know about the quality of our products. We have rallies all over the country and they bring their people. I tell them my story and unbelievable lifestyle, and share what can happen to them when they have the right attitude and desire. It helps them to see what's in store for them.

I use meetings to support, train and build my business. At home I have sales leaders who I partner with for weekly meetings, and then there's a monthly meeting at our service center. I make sure all new business builders are trained and on their way, but I refuse to manage anyone. Instead, I encourage and support them. After all, everyone is independent and in business for themselves.

The time I devote to my business varies because I can spend as much or as little time as I want. It's up to me. I know I have built a good, strong organization, and when I'm not talking and building, my people are! Something positive is always happening because that's how network marketing works. And you can rest assured there are people everywhere who need an opportunity. In fact, I find my best distributors when I least expect it.

When I approach a business prospect, I am honest, believable, excited and sincere—all at the same time. People know I am telling the truth and that I care. I let them know that if they want to build, I will do anything I can to help them. I lead with the opportunity first, while the products are always there to back me up!

One time while I was giving a lady a facial, she never smiled and didn't have anything encouraging to say. When I took off the mask I asked, "How does your face feel?" She said, "It feels funny." So I said, "That's because it has never been this clean before!" Even if I don't always say the right thing, the product always backs me up!

If, after my presentation, a person turns down my offer, it doesn't bother me. I know that every no gets me closer to a yes! If someone says no, I plant a seed. I say that if now isn't the time for them to get involved, I will still be here in the future and would love to work with them. I don't get rejections. I get postponements.

Network marketing is a business that is always opening my eyes and my heart! I remember once when I saved money for an airline ticket to take my network marketing opportunity and products home to my parents in Oklahoma. My mother was ill and listening to my presentation from her bed. She learned about our food supplements and decided to come into the business. Not long after, she regained her health and started hosting meetings herself. Eventually she and my dad became the first coordinators in the state of Oklahoma! It's memories like those that make my venture in network marketing very special to me.

Today I can honestly say I'm living my dreams! I'm sitting here on the sand at my 10,000 square foot beach home, watching the boats go by. And who would have ever thought we would have a three-story home with an elevator!

A few years ago, we took up golf. And today, we have a home on the country club with his and hers golf carts. In addition to that, my husband is a licensed skipper, so we bought a 48-foot yacht. We love sharing it with our downline, and we also enjoy fishing and taking the grandkids out.

So what's the most fulfilling part of network marketing? We have our precious time back!

The first step to succeeding in network marketing is finding the right career plan coupled with a great product. Then you combine those with lots of enthusiasm! I have learned that the biggest reason why people quit the industry is because they don't have a burning desire to do what it takes. It's a shame because you meet so many people with the talent and the needs. *But remember, you can make money or you can make excuses, but you can't make both!* Anything worthwhile takes a special effort. If you will do for two years what most people won't, you will be able to do for the rest of your life what most people can't.

To change your life, all you need to do to start is to have the right attitude. And it doesn't matter if you make a lot of mistakes. Just have a burning desire, be willing to give up something for your success, get your priorities straight and go about it!

Network marketing is growing faster than ever before. Just keep at it and you can accomplish whatever you want in life.

Don't give up on your dreams. I don't know why anyone would be satisfied with anything less than their greatest dreams. And with network marketing you can have it all!

Leslie Stanford

*"I got out of my comfort zone and did things
I never thought I could do!"*
Leslie Stanford

Background: Medical
Year started in networking industry: 1980

I was a totally broke and desperate dental hygienist when I answered an ad in the newspaper that said, "Help! My nutrition business is growing too fast for me! Need people in sales and supervisory positions." I called and spoke to a gentleman who invited me to meet with him. I assumed I was going to an interview, but it turned out to be a huge network marketing seminar. I was very turned off by that. I was clearly "too cool" to sit there and listen to a network marketing opportunity. So I tried to leave! But I couldn't because there were over 100 people in the room. It was so crowded that I couldn't get out.

I sat there really frustrated but, nonetheless, I listened. At the end of the meeting some people got up to give product testimonials. I was a little chunky and I remember thinking I wish had some money to try the product. But then I saw the income testimonials. The girl giving the meeting was a grocery checker and she was making $2,000 a month. I needed to make $2,000 in two weeks because I had no money and needed to pay my car payment and rent. So I figured that if this grocery store girl could be making $2,000 a month, I could work it twice as hard and make $2,000 in two weeks!

I was so desperate for money that I didn't have time to wait, so I signed up! I had spent all the money I had in the world to buy the business pack, which was only about $40 at the time. We met the next day and my sponsor told me what to do to get started.

I needed the money so badly and immediately that I did whatever it took to get it. I got out of my comfort zone and did things I never thought I could do!

And did I make that $2,000 in two weeks? *Yes I did!* How did I do it? I would go stand in lines at banks. I didn't have accounts at those banks, but I went there anyway. I wore a button that said, "Lose weight now, Ask me how," and it would help me to get into conversations with people. I would go up to the front of the line and then go back to the back of the line talking to everyone along the way. I spent hours doing that. It was bold and gutsy, but it worked!

When I first started my network marketing business, the money was the most fulfilling part. But today I get charged up seeing my downline get a taste of the good life. I love watching them experience what I'm experiencing. I also love seeing people get results from our products. By the way, the friendships I've made are great, too. And my sponsor is one of my best friends now.

My family and friends were very negative about my decision to get involved in a network marketing venture. I remember my dad telling me it was a scam and that I'll never make a dime. But today, every now and then he'll say, "I'm glad you didn't listen to me, Leslie!"

The thing that propels me into action is my love for my company's product line. I have 100 percent belief in them. When I hear new distributors say, "I don't care about the product, just show me the marketing plan," I always know they won't make it because there's no conviction. It's like a con to them.

Everybody has ups and downs and horrible days because network marketing is a challenge in so many ways. You might start thinking, "Maybe this isn't for me," or "It's not worth it." I almost quit many times. And it always happened that somebody would call me up and thank me for getting them involved. They would thank me for helping them lose weight and make money. So naturally I started thinking, "Well, it *is* worth it!"

In network marketing you don't have a boss and you don't have to report to work at 9 a.m. every day, so it's so easy to spend your time doing things that don't make you any money. When I first started out, I would get up late and tell myself to start working at noon. I would then go to the bank, drop off my dry cleaning, and go to the supermarket. And before I knew it, it was four o'clock and I hadn't done anything to build my business!

To combat that obstacle, I would play a mental trick on myself. I pretended I was going into work every day and that if I didn't do my job I would get fired. So I got up early every morning, worked until noon, took a lunch break, then came back and worked until evening. And when I went to bed every night I asked myself, "Would I have been fired based on my work today?" I had to be honest with myself so I could put everything into perspective. When I got focused, I lived and breathed my business and spent about 80 hours a week working it. I did get a little obsessive and would find myself up at 2 a.m., still working. Today, though, I work anywhere from 30 to 70 hours, and I love it!

Years ago we had three meetings a week, and I built my income to over a million dollars a year using that system. But today, we have technology that is just as effective, such as teleconferencing and the Internet. We still use meetings, but not on such a heavy schedule as in the past.

I use our products every day. It's part of my job description. Then I spend my time selling the product, recruiting distributors, teaching and showing my distributors how to build their businesses, and promoting events or qualifications. That's all I need to be doing. When you allow yourself to get pulled away from those things, your productivity decreases.

When approaching people about a network marketing opportunity, you need to find out what they need in life and then offer it to them. For instance, I was at a cosmetic counter today and got into a conversation with the woman who was helping me. She had a job, a husband, and a kid, and was trying to get pregnant again, so I asked her, "Who looks after your kids?" She said, "My sister-in-law watches them. She has three kids of her own, so I'm not sure how long that will last." So I said, "Well, you could do what I do! I work at home! I have three kids and working from home allows me the freedom to work around their schedules." That's the best approach. Just start a conversation based on something they can relate to. It's so easy!

Some people are interested; some aren't. At first I would cry about it after someone rejected me. I had no previous sales experience so it really hurt. But now I'm completely over that. If they say no, I know it's not me they're rejecting; it's what I'm offering them. Or maybe it's not the right time for them. If four out of ten people I talk to either buy my product or become a distributor, each no is getting me closer to a yes, right?

Everyone could be either a potential recruit or the source of a potential recruit. But, in any case, everyone can use our products. So, I approach everybody. And over the years, I have found that a lot of my distributors come from my retail customers!

When motivating my downline, I talk about the promise of the future. I encourage them to think about what could be possible for them if they got to work and built the business. Also, recognition is a great motivator. I have a top ten distributor list that I send out every week and everyone tries to get on it! People can be very competitive and recognition helps keep them motivated. If they want to quit, I remind them of why they started the business. I tell them about when I almost quit and share about others who quit and later regretted it. Promises of the future and fear of loss are powerful motivators.

I tell my distributors they need three things to be successful in network marketing. They need a product-result story, an income-result story, and a system. When I started on the products I lost 45 pounds, so I just take out my before and after photos and that will usually sell the product for me. The income-result story is what a distributor will use to recruit people into their business. If they can say to someone, "Hey, I made $328 sitting at my kitchen table today," that will get people's attention. The third thing they need to do is have a system that works for both selling the product and recruiting distributors. You need to be able to say, "Do 'x,' and 'y' will happen." If you can't show your distributors how you really build a business, they won't succeed and neither will you. You can't just say, "Go for it!" and expect it to happen automatically.

If people quit network marketing it's often because they're not making any money or they don't love the products they handle. A new person in the business needs to feel like they've got a cause—a reason to be doing this business. Without that drive, they won't sell products, they won't make money and they won't last.

We had a big event a few weeks ago and there was a distributor there who caused a lot of excitement. She finally saw her business explode—after 16 years! She hung in there and it finally took off. So the question is, "Is it worth waiting that long to make a couple hundred thousand dollars a year?" Most people would say yes.

So my advice to any new network marketer would be to never quit, unless you're in a company that has products you can't endorse or has an unproductive marketing plan. If you care more about your distributors than the money you'll make, you'll see your business grow so much faster. You deserve success and it's worth the wait!

I have a few people in my downline who, when I met them, were working in a factory assembly line. Now they're living on a beach in Malibu. Network marketing is an amazing industry. I just want to see more people succeed!

Rod T. Stinson

"So many people are out there just pitching and selling, and they don't spend enough time building relationships."
Rod T. Stinson

Background: Aerospace Industry
Year started in networking industry: 1990

Before network marketing, I was a machinist in the aerospace industry. I was sick and tired of it after only four years, but ground it out for a total of 13! I became familiar with that field so I did what most people do: I stayed in even though I didn't like it and got stuck in a rut. Then I got married and had children and started looking for different ways of making money on the side. I had done a few things but nothing that made a lot of money.

One night I worked very late, on second shift, and came home and turned on the TV at around 3 a.m. There was a little ad on the cable billboard that said, "Is what you're doing now earning you $15,000 a month?" The next day I called the number to find out what it was about. That's how I learned about network marketing. And about five years ago I found a great company and I've been with them ever since.

When I first got involved in network marketing, I told my wife, Kris, that this was the direction I wanted to go and there was no way I was going back to being a machinist. I then said to her that we may even have to go through a bankruptcy down the road to do it. Sure enough, three and a half years later we went bankrupt. And we lost everything we had, including our house and cars. Kris even lost her small hair salon business!

But my wife was wonderful about it. She was never negative nor ever told me to go back to being a machinist. Instead, she encouraged me to go forward, and stayed with and supported me, because she believed in me and that this business would work.

My family handled my decision with praise because they knew how miserable I was as a machinist. They didn't quite understand it, but they were happy I was excited about something. And again, my wife was the ultimate in support.

However, my friends were a different story. I remember my first one-on-one appointment. It was with a fellow worker I carpooled with, and worked side-by-side with for over five years. One day I finally got up the courage to talk to him about my business. His response was so negative that he tossed my opportunity information out the car window and said some things I'd rather not mention. It's easy to laugh about it now but, back then, it was tough.

Fortunately, my sponsor had prepared and informed me about the negativity I would encounter. I just didn't think it would ever be *that* bad! The funny thing is that I've been in network marketing for over nine years and to this day I've never had a reaction as negative as that one. I guess I had to get the worst one out of the way early!

In the beginning, I faced the obstacle of fear—*fear of people!* I feared what people would think and say. I was a very shy person so being in a people business was a very scary situation for me. But my dream was bigger than my reality, so I kept charging forward until those fears became my best friends. I eventually turned them around and realized that people really aren't all that bad. I found that I really do love people and enjoy working with them, but that's not where I came from initially. I have sure learned a lot about myself.

When I began to have those dreaded doubtful days that can hit every new network marketer, I'd constantly remind myself of all the other success stories I was hearing about. My mind-set was, "If they can do it, so can I." Inspirational books and tapes were also very instrumental for me when it came to removing some of my self-doubt. The key for me was to not let that self-doubt thinking stay in my head very long.

Fortunately, money isn't an issue anymore. My family and I have everything we could want. We're in the dream house we've always wanted. In fact we have three houses, cars and all that good stuff. Kris and I have been blessed with four incredible children, two boys and two girls. We have to constantly pinch ourselves when we compare where we're at to where we came from. I don't want to become complacent. I have a burning desire to continue helping the distributors in our organization get to where we are.

I get the biggest charge out of watching people grow personally, as well as seeing their incomes increase. That's what I get up for every morning. I love helping people win and bringing value to other people's lives. If you're going to get involved in this type of business, understand that other people's success is more important than your own.

We don't use alarm clocks anymore in our house! My two and three-year-olds come wake me up every morning, and I spend a big portion of the morning with them. I go into my office around 10 a.m. and start checking my faxes and messages and making phone calls. I do that until about 1 p.m., when I pick my kids up from school. I play with them for a good part of the afternoon and get back into my office around 4 p.m. I then spend a few hours on the phone doing three-way calls with my distributors. Then on Tuesdays and Thursdays you can usually find me doing presentations in a hotel. Some weeks I put in 30 hours, other weeks it's 60 to 70 hours.

When I first talk to my new distributors, I find out what they want out of their businesses. I discover their hot buttons and what things in their lives are kind of left undone. I tell them that when they build a network marketing business, they can go beyond what they ever dreamed of accomplishing. I also share with them that I believe in them. I just love helping people become successful.

I make a point of not acting like a boss. Most people come into this business part-time because they already have a full-time job and a boss they need to answer to. And the minute I sound like another boss the business begins to not be fun for them. So I would rather encourage, inspire and work with them rather than manage them. After all, nobody wants another job!

Talking to people about my business opportunity is easy. I just develop a relationship with somebody, rather than bombard them with a cold pitch. Then at some point I say something simple like, "This may sound totally off the wall, but I think I have a business you would be very interested in. Maybe in the next two or three days I'll give you call and show you a little bit of what it's about." Then, based on their response, I can begin to figure out what their hot buttons are. I think the network marketing industry gets a bad rap because so many people are out there just pitching and selling, and they don't spend enough time building relationships.

When I recruit, I like to find people who are self-motivated and want to do something with their lives. I don't like to deal with people who are negative. I'm not a convincer—that's just not me. I also make sure that the husband, the wife or the significant other are involved in what their partner is doing. Even if they're not actively involved, it's important that they at least be supportive.

My sponsor armed me with a quote that keeps ringing in my head. *"A wise person chooses carefully those whom he takes council from."* Basically, when I built my business, I only listened to the people who were successful. I never let rejection or negative opinions from others bring me down.

We need to be very cautious who we pattern our lives after and seek only those who are living the lives we want to live. It seems to be common sense, but so often we let the emotion we feel from rejection get in the way of our success. Just understand that rejection is simply a part of the personal growth process. It builds character and prepares you for the success that will follow—when you stick with it. Let's face it, this business isn't for everyone. *Some will, some won't, so what, who's next?*

The people who quit network marketing lack belief in themselves, the industry, and in other people. If the belief isn't there and they don't have a definite goal in mind that drives them, they're bound to quit. It's unfortunate, but true.

One of the first things I do with people when they join is to help them define their purpose—their reason for getting involved in network marketing. If they can give me that, I work with them. However, if they don't know the "why," even after some discussion, I won't spend one more minute with them—until they figure it out. I know it's going to be challenging for them to get motivated to even start. If they don't have that driving reason, they'll end up quitting and it will have been a waste of time for both of us.

The biggest key to success in network marketing is to be really charged up about helping people succeed. Bring them into the business, find out their reasons to succeed, and then make a commitment to help them make it happen. And it works. When you're fired up about someone else's success, they're more inclined to get excited and feel the same way. It's about helping people win! It sounds simple and it is!

No matter what anyone tells you, your success in this industry has nothing to do with where you're from, who you are, what your race is, or what your vocation, religion, or financial situation is. What matters is that you have a burning desire to make some changes in your life. I was a machinist for 13 years. My father was a machinist; my grandfather was a machinist. We were all blue-collar workers. If a guy like me can make it in this industry, I truly believe *anybody* can.

Success doesn't happen overnight. It took Kris and me five years of consistently working 10 to 15 hours a day, six or seven days a week. A lot of people think network marketers are made of something special, that they have all these unique talents and abilities, or they had a lot of money in the first place. The truth is we aren't, we don't, and we didn't. It's just a matter of being determined and persistent, and never allowing yourself to quit—no matter what obstacles you need to face and overcome. For those who win, there is no giving up.

Thousands of people's dreams are coming true because of this industry. Why not yours as well? You can do it!

Susan Waitley

"I am in love with the concept of helping as many people as possible, and that is my true passion, my true driving motivation to succeed."
Susan Waitley

Background: Homemaker, Interior Design, Medical
Year started in networking industry: 1995

Before network marketing, my full-time career had been as a wife and mother of seven. In addition to working with my husband in his business, I also renovated and remodeled homes along with doing some interior design projects. And prior to raising my family, I worked in the dental and medical field. I have always been an active person.

During the past 22 years, I accompanied my former husband to national conventions where he was a keynote speaker for many established network marketing companies. They would try to recruit us to represent them and always gave us distributor kits and products. But we always politely passed on endorsing any of those companies.

One day someone left a package at the front door that contained a supply of nutritional products, which I immediately put in the trash—with the exception of one small box. At that time eating properly wasn't a main focus due to our very heavy travel schedule—187 cities from February to November. So, I thought using the supplements might be a good idea. Soon after taking them, I noticed that I was symptom free of a 20-year health challenge. Needless to say, I was very impressed and started researching the company and its founder. I got involved because of what I learned about the science behind this company.

My family and friends have always been supportive and they, too, have joined the business. They liked me well enough before, but they love me now!

My burning drive to succeed came when I fell in love with what I was doing. I realized that, with network marketing, I was in a position to help one person who could help another, who could then help another, and so forth. I am in love with the concept of helping as many people as possible, and that is my true passion, my true driving motivation to succeed. I also want to be a role model for my daughters and other women. I want to demonstrate by example that, even when you reach your fifties, there are new horizons to explore! I want to prove that we can make a difference in the lives of the new generation, both in health and in wealth.

Self-doubt was not an issue for me. My only concern was that I had no network marketing experience. However, my belief in the quality of the products and my desire to succeed totally overcame my lack of experience. I feel as though I've reached the goals I've set for myself, but every time I reach one I raise the bar on myself. I like doing things I've never done before.

For me, overcoming fear and rejection were issues I had a tough time with. Rejection hurts at any age. I remember giving a package of information to a dear friend and I noticed her body language was as if I handed her the plague! Her reaction caused me to question why I was doing this. A few days later, she came over to my house, dropped the unopened package I had given her at my door, and drove away. I am happy to say that, over time, her husband noticed our success and asked me to show him the marketing plan. But that kind of rejection experience I had with his wife can be a big obstacle to some people.

I handle rejection now by thinking of the word no as know. In other words, they need to know more to say yes. I strive to learn more about their specific needs and provide more information. While it's true that about 97 percent of the people you talk to may not be interested the first time, 90 percent are likely to be interested the seventh! I focus on the fact that they are rejecting my presentation(s), not me personally. This helps.

Approaching prospects is not a "one-size-fits-all" thing. People are different in so many ways, and I take that into consideration with everyone I talk with. For example, when I talk with men, I use what I call the "car analogy." In many cases, men pay more attention to their cars than they do to their bodies. So I'll say something like, "We do so much preventative maintenance on our automobiles so they will perform and endure. Why not do the same for our bodies?"

I've found that women are different because we are often caretakers and, therefore, always giving. I share that if we don't take care of ourselves how can we be there to take care of others?

I lost my last grandmother last year. She had spent the last six years in a nursing home as a result of a stroke, and she hated every minute of it. I believe that if she had experienced the benefits of my company's products, she may not have had the stroke. Also, had she been the beneficiary of the income from a network marketing business, she may not have had to be in a nursing home. So, my mission now is to touch just one person's life in a meaningful way that may cause a rippling effect—the same way a stone does when it's thrown into a pond!

I like to help people improve the quality of their lives and also help them to succeed financially. It's rewarding to observe people make life decisions when money is no longer a major concern. It's very difficult to blossom personally and grow to our full potential while straining to meet our financial needs. I don't envy young families today. Women who work outside of the home, while raising a family, put in an average of 21 hours a week more than men do. So it's wonderful to watch young women succeed in a home-based business and be able to spend precious time with their families.

My days usually begin with exercise, which makes me feel refreshed and puts me in a positive state of mind. Then I go to my office and make phone calls and answer voicemails. I focus first on high-priority activities such as training and three-way calls. Every day I contact new people and send out information.

Finding new distributors is like an Easter Egg hunt—you never know where you're going to find them! I always have information with me because everyone is a prospect. When I rent a car, I leave an audiocassette in the tape deck of the car. When I am in a taxi, I leave information on the backseat. When go out to eat, I will leave a cassette with a tip. I also leave tapes in hotel rooms. When I was in Australia once, a cleaning woman from the hotel I was staying in saw some of the information, called me, and met me privately in a nearby coffee shop. She has turned out to be one of my most successful distributors. *Never* prejudge anyone!

My first home meeting was at a friend's house with six women, so we decided to turn it into a training session. Before we knew it, six turned into 18, which turned into 27. It then grew to 40, and one night we had 78 people show up! At that point we realized that 20 to 27 is the maximum number for an effective home meeting. We take reservations now and meet more frequently. We also meet about once a month for a large meeting at a hotel. Some of my best meetings are phone conferences and in Internet chat rooms.

I think it's important to empower others so you can "pass the torch." Teach your downline to run their own businesses so you don't have to do it for them. I am not responsible *for* other people. I am only responsible *to* them. I want team players who are willing to work and put forth the effort. Even if they don't produce at all, I will stick with them for about three months. You never know when someone will eventually see the opportunity and run with it!

My business is a full-time career. If you treat it like a hobby it pays you like a hobby. When you treat it like a business, though, it pays you like a business. I put in the hours because I truly love what I'm doing. And it doesn't feel like I'm working!

Persistence, consistency and passion are the keys to success. When I started in this business I was on fire, even though I didn't have any experience in or knowledge of it. All I knew was that I was going to succeed and I jumped in full speed ahead right away. If you wait until you know everything, you'll never get anything done.

The people who quit network marketing get discouraged too easily when they don't get instant results. They just don't take their businesses seriously. Network marketing is an easy business to get into. If you added three zeros to the amount of money it takes to get in, people would be more committed and treat it like a business. Also, most people don't understand the concept of residual income and prefer to go to work every day—stuck in the rut of trading hours for dollars on a fixed salary. That's simply what they're familiar with and what the people they associate with do.

To succeed in this industry, treat it like a business and respect it as a career. Work it a minimum of seven to ten hours a week, engaged in productive activities. Determine which activities produce positive results and focus only on them.

Read industry books and listen to successful network marketers with proven track records of success! Learn from them and succeed.

DREAM ACHIEVERS

When asked why new network marketers quit the industry:

37%	Expect too much too soon
27%	Fear of rejection or lack of belief in themselves
20%	Unidentified goals
10%	Lack of upline support
6%	Lack of effort

Melba and Sam Washington

"There is something special about the love, trust, loyalty, and faith we have as a family, while working with a vengeance, to reach our goals."
Melba Washington

Interview conducted with Melba only.
Background: Airline Industry, Real Estate
Year started in networking industry: 1992

S am and I were looking for an opportunity. We had lost money in both real estate and the stock market, and had been further devastated when our own business failed. We had nowhere to go but up! We needed money to pay off our debts, college tuition, and to purchase a bigger home.

It was back in 1989, while working for Singapore Airlines, that I was approached by someone I had met at a dinner party. Through his obvious knowledge, perseverance, and constant follow-up, we anxiously agreed to venture into the world of network marketing. We worked hard, but our first attempt at network marketing failed. But, fortunately, our second attempt proved to be the opportunity we had been praying for.

Our family and friends were basically supportive but they did not, in any way, mirror our excitement. We did, however, have one gutsy family member, Paulene, who for a second time joined us back in 1992. She has achieved a great deal of success in her own right, while playing a major role in ours! There is something special about the love, trust, loyalty, and faith we have as a family while working, with a vengeance, to reach our goals.

The products really amazed us, and they are what keep us continually sharing our network marketing opportunity. I had struggled with being overweight, arthritis, and back pain for years. And soon after taking our weight-loss products and herbal supplements, I got better results than I expected. In the first two weeks I lost 14 pounds, was no longer experiencing pain, and I wasn't hungry. I knew this had to be a miracle! Sam was also impressed that he had lost an inch off his waist.

We saw the potential immediately because we had already become one of our own best customers. Based on our personal experiences, the goal simply became to get as many people as possible to swallow this product as soon as we could! We knew that, inevitably, we would touch people with a product and an opportunity that could potentially change many lives.

We expected obstacles, but we had made a *solid commitment* to this opportunity and agreed that, no matter what we faced, we could handle it. A strong commitment is central to success in *any* arena.

We never had self-doubt but, without question, we did have *fear!* But since the day we started, we have been in such awe of the incredible network marketing concept. And we have always been excited by it, and had a burning desire to succeed.

We made the decision early on that we would do whatever it took as long as it was moral and ethical—regardless of the challenges. Quitting just wasn't an option. It never is for those who are serious about winning in the game of life.

We are thankful every day for being in the network marketing industry. Not only has it helped us achieve our many goals, but we have also exceeded them—*by far!* Our focus now is on helping everyone in our organization achieve what they want most. They are certainly a huge part of our lives and our success.

Time freedom is something everyone dreams of having, and we can't believe we actually have that luxury. And teaching other people how to take control of their lives, so they can have it too, is also extremely rewarding.

We strive to be givers in life, not takers. And we believe to whom much is given, much is required. We hope every day, in some way, we will be an inspiration to someone not to quit short of accomplishing their goals—to keep on persevering.

We devote many hours to working our business because we love it! We are not early risers but, when we do get up, we have a wholesome breakfast and take our herb and food supplements. Consuming our company's products every day is part of our job as distributors. We like to refer to ourselves as "products of the products."

After our prayer and meditation period, we work out at a local gym three to four days a week. Then we return to our home office to make many phone calls to our group as well as to follow up with new prospects. We also get out there and give away lots of product samples for people to try, as that's what drives our business. And, rest assured, there are lots of opportunities throughout the day to meet people—they're everywhere!

We also spend a lot of time training our downline. We work with them on all aspects of the business, but we don't manage or motivate them. Personally, I don't think external motivation has any long-term effect on people. I believe a person has to be motivated by their own burning desire to achieve their goals. Rather than attempting to motivate, we support, praise, and acknowledge their efforts and accomplishments through awards and recognition.

We also have weekly opportunity meetings where distributors can bring their guests to see a presentation. Then, once a month, we do a regional meeting. It's a four-hour "nuts and bolts" session at a large hotel.

We also hold barbecues and dinner parties in our home to recognize the people in our organization for their achievements. These events have become quite popular, as people just love to attend them.

Our approach to prospecting is to talk to as many people as possible in the course of what we do every day. We ask a lot of questions, and then listen. Our best approach is to use good *"F-O-R-M."* We ask questions about *family, occupation, recreation, and money*. Whatever our prospect needs in those areas is the focus of what we talk about. For example, we know most people have jobs they hate, so it's really easy to zero in on *that* subject! Our goal is to align our opportunity with the prospect's desires, goals and dreams. Our best distributors have come from the supermarket, bank, our vacations, and everywhere else!

Although we talk to a lot of people, we don't talk to just anybody. One of the great advantages of our business is we really do get to choose who we want to work with. Our goal is to attract honest, hardworking, caring, coachable individuals—with vision—who will take true committed ownership of their own businesses. Also, we need to like them!

We learned early on that if people weren't interested in network marketing they weren't saying no to *us*. They were saying no to the opportunity. They just didn't have a clue about how network marketing works. And while we believe we have a product everybody needs, we also know that network marketing is a numbers game. Not everyone is going say yes. But, fortunately, as successful networking professionals have proven time and time again, not everyone will be a no either!

I believe the only way to guarantee your success in network marketing is to help enough people reach their goals and you will automatically reach yours. Lead by example and never ask anyone to do anything you're not doing yourself!

Have *realistic* expectations, work diligently, and be patient—and don't expect to get rich overnight. Also, learn all you can about the industry. Read informative and inspirational books about network marketing so you can completely understand it.

Set realistic achievable goals for yourself, write them down, and review them daily. Really know your *why!* Listen to audiotapes and read books produced or promoted by industry leaders. Plug into any and all training events for which you're qualified to attend. And associate with individuals who are already successful in network marketing.

Remember, eagles don't hang out with turkeys! Set aside time for your faith and your family, and most of all, make sure you're having fun in the process!

Elizabeth Weber

"Your subconscious mind cannot tell the difference between truism and falsehood. You can either convince yourself you will make it, or convince yourself you won't."
Elizabeth Weber

Background: Secretarial
Year started in networking industry: 1982

I worked nine network marketing companies over an eleven year period before I had success in the industry. After not making any significant money over that long period of time, I had reached a point in my life where I started seriously questioning the industry.

In October of 1992 a friend approached me about the company I'm with now, and I must say I was skeptical. But as soon as I saw the compensation plan, I got really excited. I could see it was radically different than anything I'd seen before. I had finally found a company that did it right and I knew I could make a six-figure income. At the time, my husband, Bruce, was home taking care of our children. We were living on one income and had no money.

Because of the contacts I'd worn out while I was with the previous network marketing companies, I had lost my credibility. But after meeting with the corporate team, I knew this was going to be the biggest thing that ever hit this country. Something inside me told me to go for it. I caught the company's vision and quit my job of 18 years!

Everyone thought I was crazy. Nobody would listen to me. Would you listen if you knew I failed nine times before? Probably not. My husband and I had promised each other we wouldn't get involved in another network marketing company. You see, he had a front row seat to witnessing many shattered dreams and promises.

At first Bruce saw this company as just another disillusioned opportunity, but he realized it was different when I started making

221

significant money. More importantly, he saw the potential when people in my organization also started making significant money.

Before network marketing, I was sick and tired of being sick and tired! I wanted to succeed. I wanted more out of life, and a better lifestyle, with more time to spend with my family. I knew that I could do it if I just found the right vehicle.

Network marketing has allowed me to reach goals beyond my wildest dreams. I've already exceeded my personal and financial goals, and continue to set new ones. To me, network marketing isn't about the money. It's about making a difference in other people's lives. When I hit a new income level, I love to challenge myself to hit the next one to show others it's possible. I know that, in order to reach new levels, all I have to do is help others reach theirs.

Self-doubt was never an issue. I knew that if I followed the two-to-three-year business plan, I could be making six-figures with a potential of earning this income year after year. I also knew that just by helping others succeed, I would succeed because of the structure of our compensation plan.

In the beginning, it was very hard when family and friends wouldn't listen when I told them I had finally found the right company; I was going to make $2,100 a week and I could help them make it too. My back was against the wall and I knew I was going to do whatever it took to make it work. I initially got people to listen by getting them to try one of our products in the "mall without walls." Once they got incredible results from the product, they were open to listening to the business plan attached to it. Now, seven years later, I'm making $25,000 a week, and everyone's listening! Our CEO and President told me I had to succeed so that others could realize their dreams. How true!

The most fulfilling part of this business for me is being able to help others succeed and realize their dreams. I measure my success by the number of people I've helped succeed. This business has brought many people into our lives who have become lifelong friends. It has provided our family with the security and time freedom to truly enjoy our lives. Not only has it given us an incredible income, over one million dollars a year, we now have total control over how we spend our time and live our lives.

The first thing I do every day, after I get my kids off to school, is work out. It's great having a personal trainer and a home gym. I believe it's important to be physically fit as well as emotionally healthy. When I work, I do so from the comfort of my home office with the help of my assistants. I oversee the daily activities of my business, including consulting with my leaders, making three-way calls, and conducting interviews.

I enjoy doing what I do so much that I don't consider it work. It's fun and extremely rewarding. It's great to know that because of the leveraging of leadership and compounding effects of duplication, I spend many special days and nights enjoying time with my family and friends. I especially love joining my husband during the day at our golf club for a round of golf.

I motivate my organization as much as possible, but I've come to realize motivation really comes from within. I always lead by example and expect all who choose to become leaders to do the same. I empower them, set requirements and hold them accountable. But ultimately, they have to be self-motivated. It's an essential key to success.

I consistently work with my team to implement systems that duplicate. Anyone can do this business if they are coachable and willing to be a team player! I utilize all means of communication available, including our company voicemail broadcast system where I've been able to be the most creative and impactful. I have implemented what I refer to as "The Challenge Line," which gives the team a track to run on and goals to reach, stretching them to do what they need to do to succeed. It also provides incentives and recognition when they have completed the challenge.

Have you ever heard of the three-foot rule? Well, I have a ten-foot rule when it comes to prospecting. Being friendly is my nature. Anyone within ten feet is close enough for me to start a conversation and a possible relationship. But I'm quick to pre-qualify people to find out if they're right for the business. I continuously prospect, but only sponsor people who I feel will be coachable and willing to duplicate my efforts.

This business is built on developing relationships. So, as much as possible, I build a relationship first then make the approach. I use different approaches when prospecting, depending on the person and circumstances. In the beginning, I used the direct approach, which is still my most effective approach. I believe most people are looking for a better way, and I know I have what they need. The first thing I do is smile and say, "Hi." People usually respond to a smile. Then I develop a rapport by finding something we have in common or by complimenting them. There's always something nice you can say to somebody or something positive you can identify in someone.

Once I strike up a conversation, I say, "Listen, you're a people person. You'd be great in my business." And when they ask what my business is, I say, "It's a revolutionary new concept that's never been done before in the history of marketing. Let me ask you a question. If I could show you a way to earn an incredible income part-time without giving up what you're currently doing, would you take advantage of it?" That usually gets their attention. If not, they're disqualified...Next! It's a numbers game. Remember the five SWs—some will, some won't, so what, someone's waiting, somewhere.

Rejection is not an issue with me. If a person doesn't qualify, I tell them no first! I know I have what they need, whether it's financial freedom or time freedom. They need me more than I need them. The timing may not be right for them to listen. As a matter of fact, two of my top money earners said no to me for almost three years. A no is not really a no—it simply means not right now. So make sure you always follow up and respect people's timing.

When I first started my business I was so excited, and since I quit my job and my back was against the wall, I must have put in 80 hours a week. Now it's about 20 hours a week—*when I want to work*. This business has enabled us to take a lot of time off to travel, allowing us to bring family and friends along on incredible vacations. Bruce and I travel and vacation at least one week out of every month and take every holiday, school break, and summers off with our children, Bruce and Ashley. This is a dream come true!

With our success, Bruce and I went from raising our family in an 1,100 sq. ft., one-bathroom apartment, to spending quality time with our children in a 16,000 sq. ft. dream home with 11 bathrooms. Our kitchen alone is larger than our last apartment!

We've been blessed by being able to give to others because of our success in network marketing. One of my greatest joys was purchasing new cars for my dad, sister, and son. My future plans are to expand my goal of helping others in need. In 1996 I co-founded a "Bike For Life" that has raised money for charities including The Children's Wish Foundation and the American Cancer Society. My goal for the new millenium is to establish The "Weber Foundation of Helping Hands" to aid and support charities. I also plan to continue building my business—knowing that I am making a difference and that I can impact other people's lives. I'm on a mission to bring pride to the industry by helping more people than ever, in the history of network marketing, to succeed and realize their dreams.

To succeed in this business, don't waste time or try to reinvent the wheel. Work with people who really want it and are coachable and willing to duplicate your efforts. Know what your company offers and learn as much as you can. I make it a requirement for my distributors to go to all corporate events. Meetings and events are the best use of time in leveraging the growth of your business. This business is built on belief and it's the events that build strong belief systems. Always remember, "teamwork makes the dream work." So be a team player!

Your subconscious mind cannot tell the difference between truism and falsehood. You can either convince yourself you *will* make it or convince yourself you *won't*. If you think you can, you will, and if you think you can't, you're right! Go to as many events and trainings as you can to build your belief and program your mind for success. Identify someone successful in your company, make them your mentor, and simply duplicate what they do. Be enthusiastic, believe in yourself, and have a burning desire to do *whatever it takes* to succeed!

Always remember the reason *why* you're doing this business. Don't ever give up on your dreams. It's only a matter of time when your dreams will come true!

Lisa M. Wilber

*"Buckle your seatbelt
for the long haul!"*
Lisa Wilber

Background: Student
Year started in networking industry: 1991

I'm constantly advertising my company's products and business opportunity! I wear pins, shirts, and hats promoting my products. My car has my company name on its side, and a lighted sign on top that says, "To Buy or Sell." Fortunately, the company is so well-known that people walk up to me and ask about it.

One time a man saw the sign on my car and drove up beside me. He said, "I bet I make more money than you." I just happened to have a check with me and said, "Well, let's compare checks!" So he took a look and said, "Wow! I didn't know you could make $8,500 a year selling makeup!" Then I told him the check was for two weeks. And you know what? He never showed me *his* check!

My company started its network marketing program in 1992. I was doing well as a sales rep when I heard the company was launching a network marketing division. But I didn't want to do it. Many people from other network marketing companies were also pressuring me to join them. But, I thought, "This isn't me." And I believed that network marketing would actually ruin my company.

What made me change my mind was the year of research I did on the industry. I became very excited and didn't want to miss a great opportunity. So in 1993 I decided to do it. And I'm very glad I did!

When I made the announcement that I was an official network marketer, many people ridiculed me. Even today some people still think of what I do as, "Oh, there's Lisa doing her little network marketing thing." They don't view my business as real. In the beginning this caused me tremendous self-doubt. In fact, it was so great I wanted to quit every single day that first year. But I made a vow to myself that if I was going to do this I would reach the top level first before I even considered giving up. Then I could look back and see if it was all worth it. Well, it took me 15 months to make it to the top. And it *was* worth it!

My motivation to keep on going was to make a lot of money. I didn't want to ever see myself chasing the electric man around, begging him to not shut off my electricity because I couldn't pay him. But *nothing* could have ever prepared me for the fantastic money I'm making now.

When I stopped focusing on the money, I began thinking about how I could help so many other people—and that's when my mind took the big jump. So now it's the *people* I care about. For example, my company held a convention in Puerto Rico and recognized two people in my downline for their success. When they walked on stage, I cried. Knowing I had something to do with them reaching their goals has really made a difference in how great I feel about being a part of this life-growing industry.

My biggest obstacle was people not taking me seriously. For example, my mom said, "Honey, I know you're really working hard at this thing, but you're gonna have to go out and get a real job soon." I knew she cared about me, and the kicker is she works full-time for *me* now! People try to convince you it won't work. You more or less need to build an invisible fort around yourself and tell yourself that *it's going to work—no matter what.*

People ask how I run my business on a daily basis, and I always say, "I hope you're not looking for time-management tips. I wake up running and don't go to bed until I'm falling asleep standing up!" I come into my office about noon and work until 6:30 p.m., mostly on the telephone. Three employees work with me. At dinnertime I go home and spend time with my husband. After that, I go back to the office and stay there until 2 or 3 in the morning. I keep odd hours but I love it. I know I'm working hard now, but that's what will take care of me later in life.

I work about 60 hours a week even though I don't have to. But I'm having fun doing it! I'm addicted to it and over the edge!

When it comes to my downline, I believe that personal attention and recognition make for great motivators. I write a newsletter and there's a special section where I recognize my distributors for their successes.

My company holds monthly motivational meetings around the country. I also have monthly meetings at my office, and I do home meetings with my distributors from time to time. In fact, a few weeks ago I flew down to Virginia Beach for a barbecue in one of my high-level leader's backyards—and his entire downline was there! We weren't there to teach anything, just to build relationships.

What I look for in potential recruits has nothing to do with what they look like or if they're men or women. All I care about is whether they have persistence. I don't like wishy-washy prospects! I look for hardworking, enthusiastic people; and I recruit all the time.

I never try to persuade anyone to join. If they're not interested, I just say, "I'm sorry it's not right for you right now." And they often come back to me because they see it's working. Even my mom made it clear she didn't want to join. Well, about five years ago, she did. In fact, she has earned three trips and sells about $100,000 worth of product a year! But Mom changed her mind on her own, not because I was bugging her. I just share with people how happy I am about it and let them decide.

I think people quit network marketing because they don't realize how close they are to succeeding. They also can't visualize themselves becoming successful. Initially, that was hard for me too. And, if you can't visualize it, you can't make it happen.

People ask me how I succeeded, and all I can say is I never gave up. If something didn't work, I changed my approach until it did.

I also think it's important to really be in love with your products. I share them wherever I go. I wear a pin that says "I love my job," and I tell people, "The only thing I love more than my job is my boss," and I point to me! It makes people curious to find out more.

Whatever you do, don't expect to be a millionaire your first week. I tell my downline all the time that I never said it would be easy; I said it would be worth it. It's not a one- or six-month thing. Knowing that when you get started, you'll be more likely to stick with it because you'll be ready for it. So buckle your seatbelt for the long haul, and go for it!

Andy and Brenda Willoughby

"We go to bed when we want and get up when we want. We now have to read the instructions on our alarm clock if we need to use it!"
Andy and Brenda Willoughby

Background: Media, Homemaker
Year started in networking industry: 1971

Q: What did you do before network marketing?
Andy: I was a radio broadcaster. I managed radio stations and did radio programs.
Brenda: I was a homemaker and sometimes helped Andy at the radio station as the office manager.

Q: How did you get introduced to network marketing?
Andy: I was managing a television station at the time. A guy who had heard me speak at a public engagement called me and asked if I wanted to make some extra money. Next thing I knew, we were off to somebody's basement where someone explained geometric progression to us. That's what got us excited about network marketing. We did well in that first company but, unfortunately, my job eventually took me to another city and we bought a radio station. That took up a lot of our time and we stopped working our network marketing business.

Q: What happened from there?
Andy: One day, years later, I was talking to my program director and over the monitors I could hear a doctor talking about a health system. It was supposed to help everything from PMS to pimples. And I thought, "Oh no, snake oil on my radio station!" So I met with her because I thought what she was saying wasn't credible and I didn't want to offend our listening audience. But after talking to her, I thought what she was saying made sense. I didn't know much about health, but Brenda did. So I told her about it.

Brenda: At that time I had some serious health challenges, most notably asthma. I had been in and out of the hospital 23 times during the first 24 years of our marriage. I had used tried many medications and all kinds of nutritional products but none of them helped me. My health just continued to deteriorate.

The doctor from the radio station shared her products with us. But frankly, the only thing that interested me was the fact that the company offered a money-back guarantee. I went on the products and within a week I was breathing freely. And in three weeks I was off all my medications! That was such a dramatic experience for me that I got really excited about selling the products. I remembered what geometric progression was from the other company we were in and started to put two and two together. I realized I had a great opportunity in my hands, and got involved in the business and really started working at it.

Q: How did you get introduced to the company you're with now?
Brenda: We basically outgrew the second company. They had some management problems, the compensation plan wasn't as strong as we originally thought it was, and we weren't seeing the growth we wanted. That's when I started looking at other product lines. After experimenting with our current company's product line my health continued to improve. So, even though we were doing very well in that second company, we made the switch.

Q: Were your family and friends supportive of you starting a network marketing business?
Andy: We both have big families. Half of them were supportive and half weren't. Our families seemed reluctant, but the more and more Brenda and I succeeded, the more family members and friends have joined us.
Brenda: My mother is a successful network marketer, so that was a fortunate thing for us. At least we had one very supportive person on our side! In fact, she had a major influence on us to get back into the industry.

Q: What was your driving motivation to succeed in network marketing?
Andy: We had to work or starve. We put it all on the line because

we didn't have another source of income.

Brenda: We didn't like our financial situation and saw network marketing as the way out. We also wanted time freedom.

Q: Have you reached financial freedom?
Andy: It took us 25 years in the radio business to make over $100,000 a year. In network marketing, it has taken us only two and a half years to earn over $200,000 a year, and it's still growing. And our time is now our own. We go to bed when we want and get up when we want. We now have to read the instructions on our alarm clock if we need to use it!

Q: Did you ever have self-doubt and, if so, how did you deal with it?
Andy: Yes, I did. The only way to deal with self-doubt is to make more positive deposits than withdrawals to your emotional bank account. So, we bombarded ourselves with success books and motivational tapes to keep us inspired.

Q: What were your greatest obstacles?
Brenda: Fear of the phone. I was very shy. Yet I knew the telephone was my most powerful tool in making a success of myself. So I faced it head on. I set my goals and made a commitment to attain them.
Andy: Getting my momentum going was my greatest obstacle. Just getting started was a challenge! So we developed a system that is simple and easy. Once I got started dialing the phone and talking to people I was okay.

Q: What is the most fulfilling part of network marketing for you?
Andy: Every time we share our business we're excited about doing two things: We're helping people invest in both their health and their financial future. The time freedom is also a blessing. If you work for someone else, they own your time. We're enabling people to break free of that.
Brenda: We see people's health and lives change. And nothing can make us feel more emotionally fulfilled than that.

Q: Describe a typical day.
Andy: We build our downline over the telephone. We make calls

throughout the day and spend most of our evenings doing three-way calls with distributors.

Q: Describe how you motivate your downline.
Andy: We empower them with simplicity. Everybody would do network marketing if they thought they could, so we continually make things simple so people can say, "That's easy. I can do that!"

We use conference calls, simplify the presentations, have a very efficient voicemail system, and lay everything out for them. There's nothing left to figure out.

Q: Do you use meetings and events to grow your business?
Andy: We do most of our events over the telephone. We can talk to hundreds of people on one phone call and no one has to leave their house. It's efficient, cost effective, and it works.

Q: Is everyone a potential recruit for you?
Andy: We talk to everyone, but we look for people who are faithful. They also need to believe in themselves and their mission.

Q: What is your most effective approach when talking to people about your network marketing opportunity?
Andy: Honesty is the best approach. When people ask, "What do you do for a living?" I say, "I'm in network marketing!" I'm shouting it from the rooftops now because I'm so thrilled with my life!

Why wouldn't *anyone* want to live the same lifestyle Brenda and I live? If everyone in network marketing ran around with a T-shirt on that said, "I'm in network marketing," it would generate tremendous interest from people who aren't in yet, right? Why is everyone keeping it a secret? I'm proud and excited about it!

Q: How do you deal with rejection?
Andy: At first, when someone said no my thought process was, "I'll talk them into it yet!" I considered it a challenge worthy of my time. But today I move them to the three-month file. I call them back every three months until they agree to hear me out.
Brenda: I used to take rejection personally. It took me a very long time to figure out they weren't rejecting me; they were rejecting my opportunity.

Q: How much time do you commit to your business every week?

Andy: Building a network marketing business is like flying a rocket ship. If you want it to take off you'd better put out a lot of thrust in the beginning.

Brenda: I was putting in 60 hours a week and Andy was putting in time as well. Today it varies between 20 and 40 hours a week.

Q: What are the keys to success in network marketing?

Andy: We have a three-step process. We let the company literature and tapes sell the products, the upline sells the opportunity, and we make the contacts.

Brenda: Another key is consistency. There are people who get involved, work hard and diligently for three months, and then quit. Or, they'll work for two weeks and quit for three. They need to work it every day to see results. But they don't need to kill themselves—just keep working at it. A steady pace brings prosperity.

Q: Why do you think people quit network marketing?

Brenda: They don't know what to do so they don't do anything.

Andy: The only reason why someone wouldn't do network marketing is because they don't think they can! If they really think they can do it, they'll do it. It's a belief challenge.

Q: What advice could you give to people who are just starting out in network marketing?

Brenda: Be consistent and stick around!

Andy: You need a balance in your life. Don't get involved and work so hard that you burn out. There is a learning curve to network marketing and it takes a little time. But eventually you will build belief in yourself and what you can accomplish. Take it one step at a time and be teachable! You can do it.

DREAM ACHIEVERS

FACTOID #10

How did the Dream Achievers deal with rejection when prospecting?

100% Maintained a Positive Attitude

48% Said that prospects don't reject people... they reject what is being offered

38% Said prospecting is simply a sorting process... nothing more, nothing less

14% Said persistence can overcome rejection over time

The End of the Rainbow

"You can't have a rainbow without first some rain."

When we first got involved in network marketing in 1997, we saw the opportunity to control our destinies. Our belief that we could be successful with this vehicle overpowered our fears. We shared this business with all of our friends and family members, and put in many hours a week prospecting and running meetings. We also used the products and invested in books, tapes, and seminars to grow ourselves as well as our business. We just knew our commitment would reward us someday. We had dreams and absolutely no one was going to prevent us from achieving them.

We were revved up and working harder than ever before to make our dreams come true. And, just like everyone else in network marketing, or any business for that matter, we had our moments of serious frustration. Then one day, we started talking about how valuable it would be to read a book about people from all walks of life who succeeded in this business. We weren't interested in a "how to" book per se; instead, we wanted to immerse ourselves in a collection of inspiring conversations with some of the leaders in the industry. We searched for months but couldn't find anything anywhere that fit this description. We were honestly shocked! We couldn't imagine the ever-growing network marketing industry *without* this kind of book. So we decided to write it ourselves.

We wanted to create a book that would inspire network marketers when they got frustrated. We wanted to create a book that would remind them that the opportunity network marketing offers is truly a wonderful gift—*like a beautiful rainbow*.

When a rainbow appears, it seems to force you to pay attention to and appreciate the beauty around you, rather than take it for granted. When that multi-colored arc lights up the sky, doesn't virtually everyone who notices it stop what they're doing to admire it? You may even see drivers pulling over to the side of the road and taking pictures. You'll probably see people smiling and pointing and absorbing the magnificent scene. And when it finally disappears, those who were fortunate enough to spot it feel lucky to have witnessed this seemingly miraculous event.

That same feeling is what we hope this book has generated in you, as well as in the hearts of millions of network marketing prospects and distributors around the world.

Not surprisingly, most of the companies we contacted were more than willing to have their leaders participate. We suddenly found ourselves with a huge list of people to interview. And we received over a hundred phone calls from leaders, as well as from companies who also wanted their leaders to be included in the book! We were excited.

We continued to diligently build our network marketing business and write this book at the same time. We were finally on the road to controlling our destinies *and* sharing the beauty of the network marketing industry. Our heads were spinning. Life couldn't have been better!

And then, about three months later, we were faced with some serious challenges of our own—the details of which aren't important. The wonderful thing is—*the inspiration we gained from the interviews with the leaders in this book kept us going.* And they can do the same for you!

After talking with so many truly successful people, some of whom endured far worse difficulties than any of our challenges, we realized, first-hand, that our efforts were worth it. We wanted to provide a book that would motivate new, as well as seasoned, network marketers—*and we got motivated in the process.*

What validation—*the book did what it was envisioned to do!*

We knew that many of our difficulties were just small hurdles. They really didn't change the fact that we still had dreams to achieve—*and that we could still accomplish what we set out to do.*

How could we forget the words of Roland Fox who said he had tried 25 different opportunities before he finally succeeded in network marketing? How could we ignore Lydia Chan's success, a woman who spoke little English? Or how about the late Ken Pontious? His father had constantly put him down and told him he would never be successful at anything. He, of course, then went on to achieve more than he could possibly imagine in network marketing?

What about Lisa Wilber, the woman who wanted to quit every day her first year—but stuck it out and is now happier than ever? And how could we not remember the success story of J.K. Baker? He said his banker laughed in his face when he talked about getting into network marketing. And what about the other 45 people we interviewed?

Since they did it, so could we—*and you can too!*

Our only recourse was to forge ahead and continue on our journey, in spite of the roadblocks that seemed to be in our way. We took the advice of these Dream Achievers. We were committed to sharing with our readers that they need to have the faith that they *can* achieve their dreams—regardless of the obstacles they need to overcome. When you have a chance to control your destiny, like network marketing enables you to do, think about what Jan Ruhe says, "You can either jump on the ship or watch it sail by."

We have overcome one of the greatest challenges of our lives, and are now going strong again. We are, once more, excited about our futures and on our way to achieving our dreams. How about you?

Writing *Dream Achievers* was truly a labor of love. We have made many new friends along the way and are thankful for their generous contributions to this book. Their pioneering wisdom will continue to enlighten us as we journey on to find our dreams at the end of the rainbow. And we hope they will do the same for you!

So, get a grip on your dream and start building your own network marketing business. Use this book to help you find others who will want to join you, as well as to help inspire those in your group. Who knows? Before too long, you, too, could be a Dream Achiever. And maybe we'll interview *you* someday to be in a future edition!

Go for it. *You can do it!*

Go for it,

Anthony and Erik Masi

DREAM ACHIEVERS

What motivated the Dream Achievers
to succeed in network marketing?

42%   Desire for time
         freedom

40%   Extra income / to
         get out of debt

18%   Helping others
         improve the quality
         of their lives

About the Authors

Anthony and Erik Masi are twin brothers who grew up in West Hartford, Connecticut. *Dream Achievers* is their first book.

Anthony holds a B.A. in English with a concentration in Writing from Fairleigh Dickinson University. Before *Dream Achievers,* he spent years performing on college campuses as a professional magician. His love for the creative arts has also stemmed into songwriting and screenwriting, and he is also a certified handwriting analyst.

Erik has attained a B.S. in Management from Bryant College and has over a decade of experience in the direct sales industry. He is also a motivational speaker and business owner.

Their venture into network marketing has been a life-changing experience. They created *Dream Achievers* to share the beauty of the network marketing industry with you.

"If you can dream it, you can do it."

Walt Disney